The former Yugoslavia in 1991
(after the dissolution of Yugoslavia and
before the Dayton peace accord)

Royalties from this book will be distributed to projects that work with refugees and displaced people in the countries of the former Yugoslavia. Decisions on distribution will be made locally by a geographically and nationally diverse committee composed of women's organizations working with refugees, including Medica/Women's Therapy Center, Zenica; Duga, Women's Center, Banja Luka; Center for Women War Victims, Zagreb; Autonomous Women's Center, Belgrade. For more information, contact Rada Boric, Center for Women War Victims, Dordiceva 6, 41000 Zagreb, Croatia. To be included in a follow-up report on The Suitcase, *or to create a Suitcase in another part of the world, contact Julie Mertus, Harvard Law School, 401 Pound Hall, Cambridge, MA 02138, USA; e-mail: suitcase@igc.apc.org.*

THE

TRANSLATIONS BY

Jelica Todosijevic

Rada Boric

Jasminka Kalajdzic

Vinka Ljubimir

Andrea Matacic

Vanda Perovic

Slavica Stojanovic

Jasmina Tesanovic

SUITCASE

REFUGEE VOICES FROM BOSNIA AND CROATIA

With contributions from over seventy-five refugees and displaced people

EDITED BY

Julie Mertus

Jasmina Tesanovic

Habiba Metikos

Rada Boric

TEXT EDITORS

Julie Mertus

Jasmina Tesanovic

STORY SELECTION

Habiba Metikos

Rada Boric

FOREWORD BY

Cornel West

AFTERWORDS BY

Dubravka Ugresic

Marieme Helie-Lucas

Judith Mayotte

UNIVERSITY OF

CALIFORNIA PRESS

BERKELEY

LOS ANGELES

LONDON

Support for collecting the stories in The Suitcase *was provided in part by Oxfam, a British-based international humanitarian aid organization presently working with refugees and displaced people throughout the former Yugoslavia as well as in other countries; its mission is to achieve basic rights and sustainable livelihoods regardless of ethnicity, religion, gender, physical abilities, or sexual orientation.*

University of California Press
Berkeley and Los Angeles, California

University of California Press, Ltd.
London, England

Library of Congress Cataloging-in-Publication Data
The suitcase : refugee voices from Bosnia and Croatia /
    edited by Julie Mertus . . . [et al.] ; foreword by Cornel
    West ; with contributions from over seventy-five
    refugees and displaced people, and Dubravka
    Ugresic . . . [et al.] ; translations by Jelica
    Todosijevic . . . [et al.].
        p.   cm.
    Includes bibliographical references.
    ISBN 0-520-20458-1 (cloth : alk. paper);
    ISBN 0-520-20634-7 (pbk: alk. paper)
    1. Yugoslav War, 1991– —Refugees. 2. Yugoslav
War, 1991– —Personal narratives, Bosnian. 3. Yugoslav
War, 1991– —Personal narratives, Croatian.
4. Forced migration—Yugoslavia—History—20th
century. 5. Refugees—Bosnia and Hercegovina—
Biography. 6. Refugees—Croatia—Biography.
7. Bosnia and Hercegovina—History—1992– .
8. Croatia—History—1990– . I. Mertus, Julie, 1963– .
II. West, Cornel.
DR1313.7.R43S85   1997
949.702′4—dc20   96-18199

Printed in the United States of America
9 8 7 6 5 4 3 2 1

Za mir
(for peace)

CONTENTS

F rom letting us sleep on their floors, to publicizing this project and helping us reach refugee authors, to translating and delivering articles into our hands, many people have helped us with this project. In particular, we wish to thank our literary agent, Ellen Geiger, and our editor at the University of California Press, Naomi Schneider, for believing in the importance of refugees' voices; Cornel West, Dubravka Ugresic, Marieme Helie-Lucas, and Judith Mayotte for sharing their words with us; and the many regional photographers who shared their pictures. We are grateful to Oxfam for facilitating the collection of stories, and to Kathleen MacDougall, Dore Brown, and Nola Burger at the University of California Press for the careful attention they paid to these stories. Also, the John D. and Catherine C. MacArthur Foundation and the Soros Foundation supported Julie Mertus's year-long stay in the former Yugoslavia, which was crucial in completing this work. And, above all, this work could not have been completed without the help of Jelica Todosijevic and Slavica Stojanovic. In addition, we wish to acknowledge the support of the following people and organizations (in alphabetical order): Amra and Enes, Bosnian Club of St. Louis, Mo.; Autonomous Women's Center, Belgrade; Genc Bucinca, Pristina, Kosovo; Rev. Klaus Burckhardt, Hermannsburg, Germany; Anna Cataldi, Milan, Italy; Bosfam, Tuzla, Bosnia-Herzegovina; Carnegie Endowment for International Peace, Washington, D.C.;

Center for Women War Victims, Zagreb, Croatia; Amela Curkovic, Zagreb; Eve Ensler, New York; Judit Hatfaludi, American Friends Service Committee, Budapest; Joanna Howlett and Murph Ehman, Buffalo, N.Y.; Jagoda Hozo Lazarevic, The Czech Republic; HR-NET (Debra Guzman); Human Rights Watch, Helsinki, based in New York; International Organization for Migration (IOM), Geneva and Belgrade; *Izi: Refugees for Refugees,* Ljubljana, Slovenia; Indira Kajosevic, New York; Women, Law and Development, International, Washington, D.C.; Jesuit Refugee Service—Europe, Brussels; Katrin Kremmler, Berlin; Vinka Ljubimir, New York and Dubrovnik; Medica Zenica, Zenica, Bosnia-Herzegovina; Lepa Mladjenovic, Belgrade; Marilyn and Daniel Mertus, North Carolina; Zoran Mutic, Ljubljana; Odgovor, Humanitarian Information Center, Belgrade; Marta Pardavi, Helsinki Committee, Budapest; Refugees from Bosnia and Herzegovina Association, Osijek, Croatia; Ursula Renner, Nuremberg, Germany; Sonia Jaffe Robbins, New York; Rosa House, Zagreb; Inga Saffron, Moscow; Barbara Schiestl, Vienna; Haya Shalom, Jerusalem; Svetlana Slapsak, Ljubljana; Soros Fond Jugoslavija (especially Sonja Licht), Belgrade and Pristina; Jovanka Stojsavljevic, Oxfam, Zagreb; UNHCR, Geneva, Zagreb, and Belgrade; Rachel Wareham, Zagreb; Women in Black, Belgrade; Women in Black, Jerusalem; Women in Black, New York; Women's Committee for Refugee Women and Children, New York; Women Living Under Muslim Laws, France; ZAMIR (e-mail network for activists in ex-Yugoslavia); Eva Zillen, Kvinna till Kvinna, Sweden; Mary Zirin, Women East-West, Altadena, Calif.

The following contributions are reprinted with permission:

From *Izi: Refugees for Refugees* (Ljubljana, October 1993 and October 1994)

> Ferida Durakovic, "Every Mother Is a Gifted Child"; Tomaz Jurancic, "No Title"; Almina Kotoric, "If I Were an Apple"; Mujo Mustafic, "You Won't Find Me Here"; Mirjana Nuspahic, "From Day to Day"; Mirsada Salihovic, "I Wish I Had a Mask"

From *New Internationalist,* no. 270 (August 1995): 12–13

> Rada Boric, "The Oasis"

From *Sarajevo: Voci da un assedio,* ed. Anna Cataldi (Milano: Baldina and Castoldi, 1993)

> Anon., "Letter to My Daughters"; Edina, "Ruins"; Zana, "When Father Is in War"; Zehra, "Dear Cousin Jasmin"

A s we approach the end of this ghastly century, we wonder whether we can hold on to those ideals—or illusions?—that give such meaning, purpose, and order to the wretched world we inhabit. Nearly 200 million fellow human beings have been murdered in this dreadful century in the name of some vicious ideology. Nazism at the heart of so-called civilized Europe. Stalinism at the core of the so-called emancipatory Soviet Union. European and Japanese imperialism in Africa and Asia. Patriarchal violence in the domestic sphere. Homophobic attacks in public places.

The problem of evil—of unjustified suffering, unmerited pain, and undeserved harm—remains the problem of the twentieth century. And the plight and predicament of refugees from Bosnia-Herzegovina and Croatia make this suffering, pain, and harm concrete in a frightening way. For four excruciating years, these overwhelmingly civilian victims of bloodthirsty armies have been degraded, dishonored, dislocated, and displaced. And the world has looked at this appalling mistreatment with both horror and complacency. Horror in that such inhumanity to people is atrocious. Complacency in that so few world leaders are willing to stop it.

In this unique book, which includes from all ethnonational groups poignant stories brought together by a team of editors representing all these groups, we move from the searing headlines about the people to the courageous voices of the people. We hear their powerful words in ways they define under circumstances defined by others. We are deeply moved by their precious memories under pernicious realities created by others.

In short, we witness the spiritual strivings of a downtrodden yet dignified people whose will to persist and prevail is so nobly evident. In the midst of such sadness and sorrow, these fellow human beings—refugees coping with so much misery—refuse to allow misery to have the last word. Such gestures of hope grounded in everyday struggle keep alive the most precious gems of life—love and faith. Let us pledge to remain in solidarity with such hope for refugees and displaced people around the world.

OPENING THE SUITCASE

We have heard all about the shelling of Sarajevo, scanned headline after headline on the destruction of "Yugoslavia," and watched endless television coverage of civilians dodging bullets and fleeing destroyed lives, but we haven't heard the voices of refugees. "When you're a refugee, nobody asks you how you are," one Bosnian refugee confided. She was from a Muslim community.[1] And she spoke from a refugee camp in Pakistan. But she could have been from Croatian or Serbian communities, and she could have been in Croatia or Bosnia or Serbia, or in any European or American country. She could have even been a refugee from another con-

---

1. We prefer where possible to identify people as being from "Muslim, Croatian, and Serbian communities," instead of as being "Muslim, Croat, or Serb" in recognnition of the complex nature of identification of self and other, particularly here, where in a large number of families there are intermarriages, and where many people do not in fact identify themselves monolithically as Serb or Croat, or Muslim, at least not before the war began. Before and even now, many refugees identify themselves according to place and not to ethnic group, or at the very least according to group and place—i.e., Bosnian Muslim, Bosnian Croat, Bosnian Serb. The matter becomes more confused with the term "Muslim" as the word also refers to a religion, but Muslims of Bosnia-Herzegovina are rarely religious and most have little in common with those who practice the religion of Islam elsewhere (see afterword by Marieme Helie-Lucas). To the extent that "Muslim" is used here, the term refers to people who are identified with that ethnonational group.

flict, in Haiti or Rwanda perhaps. When you're a refugee, no matter who you are, nobody asks, "How are you?"

This book asks refugees[2] from Bosnia-Herzegovina and Croatia this simple question. Here, refugees tell their own stories about their lives *as refugees* in their own voices, through stories, essays, poems, and letters.

In some ways, we are all refugees, if only for a moment. Remember that feeling of loneliness, as if a child uprooted from all things known and unknown, of cosmic displacement, as if an alien on an unknown planet. Then imagine freedom beyond the limit of human need, freedom from context, freedom from life itself—freedom as a personal enemy, bare and raw, imposed by outside forces suddenly and without warning. Being a refugee is the other side of being human, its dark side.

We are all born into a history, but refugees, torn from their homes and cast out of their histories, are forced into the thorny pass of saints. As they gather the threads of their past lives and wait to begin again, refugees all come to the same, often unspoken, realization: All people are kin even if they kill each other, and especially if they kill each other since they all lie in the same graves; there is no just cause, just war, or victory where the loot is only material or the gain is power over another; there are no religious, ethnic, or political differences as great as the gap between pain and joy, war and peace, life and death. This revelation may be worth sacrifice, but we could avoid repeating the sacrifice if only we listened to the wisdom of refugees.

Many Europeans and Americans, soaked in their own prejudice and ignorance, may try to dismiss refugees from Asia and Africa as a distant "other"—a creature foreign from and opposite to themselves. But they can see themselves in the refugees from Bosnia-

---

2. As explained below, we use a lay person's definition of refugee, not the legal definition. All people who left their community and considered themselves refugees were eligible for this collection.

Herzegovina and Croatia. These are people from small European towns and cosmopolitan cities who have lost their ski vacations, compact discs, and VCRs. Newspapers may love to display photographs of old farm ladies with scarves on their heads—and indeed many refugees from Bosnia-Herzegovina and Croatia[3] are old and some do wear scarves—but many more refugees are young cosmopolitans. Perhaps if readers begin to relate to this refugee population as themselves, they would begin to feel the needs of other refugee populations as well. All refugees, no matter what race, ethnicity, religion, or geographic location, are "us."

Popular opinion has turned against refugees, as their numbers worldwide have swollen from 2.5 million in 1970 to over 23 million today.[4] And the number of "displaced people"—people who have fled their homes but who remain in their countries of origin—has reached over 25 million.[5] In World War I, only 5 percent of casual-

3. In line with the wishes of the majority of refugee authors to this collection and unless the authors expressly refer to a different term, we use throughout the names of the internationally recognized countries (Bosnia-Herzegovina, Croatia) and refer to the larger, prewar territory of Yugoslavia as ex-Yugoslavia or the former Yugoslavia. We use "reduced Yugoslavia" when referring to the only two parts of the former Yugoslavia that remain together and call themselves Yugoslavia. Few people, with the exception of the foreign news media, use the term "former Yugoslavia" to describe the presently existing countries (just as no one, apart from the foreign news media, refers to Russia, Ukraine, or the other newly independent states as "the former Soviet Union"). Even those disagreeing with the use of the terms "Croatia" and "Bosnia-Herzegovina" do not suggest the term "former Yugoslavia." (For example, residents of the formerly Serbian-populated and Serbian-controlled territory in southern Croatia known as "Krajina" referred to their land not as "former Yugoslavia" but as the "Serbian Republic of Krajina.")

4. In the middle of 1995, the UN High Commission on Refugees estimated the number of refugees worldwide at 23 million. UNHCR, Office of the Special Envoy for former Yugoslavia, Briefing Kit (March 1995). See also UNHCR, *Information Paper 1994*, and UNHCR, *The State of the World's Refugees* (New York: Penguin Books, 1993), which sets the number of refugees at the end of 1992 at 18.2 million.

5. Estimate drawn from interviews with the International Working Group on Refugee Women, Vienna, February 1995; UNHCR field offices, Zagreb and Belgrade, February and March, 1995; and Women's Commission for Refugee Women and Children, New York, February 1994.

ties of war were civilians and 95 percent were combatants; today the numbers are reversed: 95 percent of casualties of war are civilians and only 5 percent are combatants. Despite these statistics, European countries have erected new barriers to refugees, issued new visa requirements, built new border crossings, held meeting after meeting to discuss refugee and immigration controls without even putting "how to help refugees" on the agenda. Xenophobia has intensified and few countries have done anything to stem the tide of ignorance and hate.

Dehumanized and defaced, refugees become a suitable scapegoat, especially in countries facing their own ethnic and racial tensions and economic crises. The refugees from Bosnia-Herzegovina and Croatia, like other refugees throughout time and across continents, are in danger of being treated as mere refuse from a war we would rather forget.

Learning the Power of Refugees' Voices

This project has forced us, the editors, to push ourselves beyond our own despair, which we experienced in different ways and varying degrees but which drove us all to do something to fight the insanity surrounding us. We began this project separately and then came together as our paths converged through our work. One of us was a human rights lawyer, working on war crimes evidence and the gathering of stories of human rights abuses in ex-Yugoslavia. Her task was to focus on the human rights violations themselves and to put her pen down when refugees began talking about their lives after the abuses stopped. In the middle of some of this work, Bosnian refugees in Zagreb gave her a bundle of handwritten stories about their lives *as refugees* and pleaded with her to do something with them. She promised she would do her best.

Few newspaper editors were interested in these stories—only the most immediate crimes and the most pitiful accounts could catch their eye. But these refugees were not pitiful, nor were they asking for pity. They just wanted to tell their stories with dignity and pride. The human rights lawyer contacted her friends and colleagues in Zagreb and Dubrovnik for their assistance, and two members of the Center for Women War Victims in Zagreb came into the project: one woman from Zagreb and another woman from Bosnia-Herzegovina (herself a refugee). Potential contributors were told to focus on what had happened to them from the point at which they fled their homes and, if possible, to describe a single event, a single day, a single feeling. The stories started trickling in; about 10 percent were usable.

Then at a women's studies conference in Belgrade in June 1994, a beautiful reading on refugees by a feminist author caught the human rights lawyer by surprise. The refugee book needed help. By some coincidence, the feminist author was planning to produce a similar collection of refugee writings. She had heard of the lawyer's work and had been looking for her. Could they all work together? Our collaborative effort began that day.

Yet we had already been collaborating for some time with dozens of people throughout all parts of ex-Yugoslavia and abroad, some of whom we've never even met in person but were connected with via electronic mail.[6] While we traveled extensively in search of stories, we were not able to reach every area in person. Thus, we also relied on contributions sent through electronic mail networks, mailings,

---

6. The failure of electronic mail is a story of the war and refugees in and of itself. When phone lines were cut at the beginning of the war, e-mail provided the only direct link between Croatia and Serbia and many parts of Bosnia-Herzegovina. In Belgrade, however, the entire e-mail system collapsed in the summer of 1995 when the system became overburdened and then one of the three main operators became a refugee in New Zealand and another, a refugee from Sarajevo, went into hiding to avoid being sent back to fight. Due to this failure, nearly all stories that had been coming from refugees in England and Australia were lost. But electronic mail is not the only kind of mail that fails. Long after this manuscript was completed, several contributions sent via regular mail arrived at the editors' door. Some had been traveling for nearly a year, having been bounced back and forth between Europe and the United States before finally finding the intended recipient.

and personal contacts with refugee and humanitarian aid organizations in Slovenia, Croatia, Bosnia-Herzegovina, Serbia, and
elsewhere; journalists; peace and human rights groups; and, most
important, refugee-run magazines and other refugee-run organizations. Our policy was simple: look for contributions everywhere and
read everything sent to us.

This is not and has never been a scientific study or a representative
sample. An ad hoc collection of stories, this book presents small cor-
ners of a many-angled refugee population scattered throughout the
globe. This work includes only the few we could reach on a budget
of zero, the few who could somehow put aside the trial of everyday
survival, the few who could or would remember. While scientific
studies lose their importance over time and today's statistics are replaced by those of tomorrow, these stories, as pieces of literature and
memories of witnesses, will never lose their importance.

Also, this book is not a collection of testimony for a war crimes
tribunal or other court. While some of these stories speak about potentially prosecutable crimes, most of them point mainly to the destruction of the human spirit—alone an offense for which there is
no law. The purpose for which these stories were gathered is not the
same as that of investigators working for a war crimes tribunal or
other court. We weren't trying to prove a crime against an individual
based on a set evidentiary standard. We didn't "examine" the refugees. In fact, we didn't ask many questions at all. We just asked
refugees if they wanted to talk or write about their experiences *as
refugees*. At times we gave an assignment, such as "Write about what
you remember from home." Then we collected the stories without
judgment, selecting them based on how well they contributed to
telling the story of refugee life to outsiders.[7]

---

7. We sought out stories from all ethnonational groups. When we recognized
there was a paucity of stories from Croat refugees, we deliberately sought additional
contributions from members of that group. However, apart from this effort, we
never asked the ethnonational group of the contributor. (While we could tell some-

In our approach, we do not seek to make refugees into an "Other," an "object [to be] appropriated, interpreted, taken over by those in power, by those who dominate."[8] Here refugees are the subject, not the object. To the greatest extent possible, they are to maintain control over royalties from their words, and they are the ones who have directed the content of this project. The stories were written by the refugees themselves or, when refugees found it too difficult to write, the stories were told to the editors and later transcribed. Nearly all refugees chose to begin or end their essays with memories of the peaceful life they left behind; many of them lament the multiethnic society that was and may never be again. Some pledge to return as soon as possible; some swear they could never return; most wish they could return to the old life they've left behind. We kept some of these introductions and conclusions in full; we edited some for the sake of space and repetition. In doing so, we have striven to publish the refugees' stories in as full and honest voice as possible.

Julie Mertus added commentaries at the end of each piece to provide context—to tell a little more about the individual if she or he so desired, the process by which the story was solicited (in particular, acknowledging where the testimonies are mediated), and to provide some factual grounding for readers who have less knowledge about the war.[9] We included more factual notes in the beginning stories to enable all readers to gain entry, and we presented facts in piecemeal

times from the last name, we could not detect "mixed families," nor did we seek to do so, unless the contributor volunteered that information.) The bulk of the stories appear to be from Muslim refugees. To the extent that our collection of stories is not representative of the entire refugee population, it is probably still for a lack of stories by Croats, despite all our efforts.

8. bell hooks, *Yearning: Race, Gender and Cultural Politics* (Boston: South End Press, 1990), 125 (commenting on the phenomena of privileged self and the "Other" in the work of white scholars writing about black people).

9. The factual material in the explanatory notes is drawn from *Economist* and *New York Times* articles, as well as the excellent chronology of events compiled by Samantha Powers for the Carnegie Endowment entitled "Breakdown in the Balkans: A Chronicle of Events, January, 1989 to May, 1993" (Carnegie Endowment Special Publication, undated).

fashion, much as one lives a life. The location cited in the identification line at the beginning of each piece is the home place from
which the contributor fled. The location cited at the end of each
piece is the place where it was spoken or written; the date the piece
was composed is also noted.

We who are not refugees recognize our outsider status and the
privilege we have in being able to fly into the war zones, visit refugee
camps, sit in refugees' kitchens—and then return to our homes of
safety and comfort. At times, we have been paralyzed by this privilege. How could we possibly do justice to these stories? When an
eleven-year-old girl tears the only copy of her favorite poem out of
her notebook and hands it to us, when our tape recorder dies in the
middle of an interview with a rape survivor and the young woman
insists on retelling her horror so we can get every word exactly right,
when an old man forces himself to remember something he has
taken months to try to forget—when we enter other people's lives
and dreams, we undertake a serious responsibility. And we know it.
We are grateful to the refugees who have chosen to tell their stories
and we respect those who've chosen to remain silent.

Defining "Refugee": The Scope of the Collection

In this collection, we have included stories of unregistered and registered refugees (registered with UNHCR, the UN High Commission on Refugees, or the host country). The only criteria is that
the person fled from their home in Croatia or Bosnia-Herzegovina
and that they consider themselves to be refugees. Thus, we use the
everyday understanding of the term "refugee": anyone uprooted
from their home because of violence and the denial of human
rights. Under international law, however, the definition narrows.
According to the 1951 UN Refugee Convention, "refugees" include
only those who flee persecution (based on specified factors such as
ideology and ethnicity) in their home countries. Those who flee but
do not cross country borders are deemed "displaced people," not

refugees. Also excluded from refugee status under the Convention are all who cannot demonstrate that they face persecution *as individuals* and those fleeing economic conditions and general political upheavals.

People fleeing conflict do not register themselves as refugees for several reasons. Often they cannot do so because they have not crossed an international boundary. This is particularly the case in Croatia. While Croatia has accepted over 300,000 official refugees from Bosnia-Herzegovina, the state also must cope with an equal number of internally displaced people who fled one part of Croatia for another. Although they fled because their old homes were taken over by Serbian people who declared a new state, their claims to a new state have not been internationally recognized (and certainly not by Croatia) and thus they are not technically refugees. Fear of ill-treatment by the receiving country also may cause some refugees not to register themselves. For example, some Bosnian Muslims who fled to Serbia told us they feared persecution by the Serbian regime; some male Bosnian Serbs who fled to Serbia told us they feared being sent into the Bosnian Serb army. At the same time, some Bosnian Muslims who fled to Croatia feared being sent back home too early; and Bosnian Muslims in Switzerland and other countries said they feared being sent back because they had never followed the proper procedures for entering the country legally as a refugee.

While we do not observe the legal distinction between "refugee" and "displaced person" here, we understand the importance of legal refugee status. Persons with official refugee status enjoy greater international protection under the law, including protection from being forced back to their homes when they would still be placed in danger and protection from being drafted into military service in their host country. Refugees from Bosnia-Herzegovina and Croatia have faced both of these concerns. Serbia, for example, has attempted to force refugees who are living in Serbia to return to their homes or to other communities in Bosnia-Herzegovina, even when hostilities have not ended there, apparently to force them to fight for the territory. In a more blatant move, some male Bosnian Serbian refugees living in refugee camps in Serbia have reported receiving call-up notices for the Bosnian Serb army. If these refugees do not have official refugee status, they cannot rely on international protection. Many authors who did not sign their pieces under their real name are not official refugees.

At the time these stories were written, the authors were in refugee camps or other temporary or semipermanent quarters throughout all of ex-Yugoslavia, and in such diverse locations as Pakistan, Turkey, Israel, The Czech Republic, Hungary, Austria, Germany, Italy, England, and the United States. While this list of countries is extensive, it is far from exhaustive. Refugees from Bosnia-Herzegovina and Croatia have fled to over four times as many countries as we have represented here.

Bosnia-Herzegovina has the greatest share of displaced people. According to the UN High Commission on Refugees and local refugee offices, in mid-1995, there were nearly three million refugees and displaced people in Bosnia-Herzegovina—over half the population—and over three-quarters of the population was dependent on humanitarian aid for basic survival.[10] During the same time period, the Office for Displaced Persons and Refugees of Croatia placed the number of refugees and displaced people in Croatia at 385,000—roughly 8.5 percent of the population; the Ministry of Labor in the ex-Yugoslav Republic of Macedonia set the number at 15,000 refugees—about 0.7 percent of the population; the Slovenian Red Cross counted 28,000 refugees—1.3 percent of the population; and the Serbian Commissioner for Refugees and the Montenegrin Red Cross estimated over 400,000 refugees and displaced people— 4.3 percent of the population.[11]

10. UNHCR, Office of the Special Envoy for former Yugoslavia, Briefing Kit (March 1995), 17.

11. Ibid. Note that all these statistics are from governmental sources and UNHCR, and that UNHCR counts only recipients of its aid; it relies on govern-

In August 1995, after this mid-year survey, the number of refugees
in Serbia swelled when Croatian troops reclaimed the rebel southern
Croatian territory that had been populated and controlled by Croatian Serbs (an area known as the Krajina), forcing over 250,000
Croatian Serbs to leave their homes on the same day, flooding the
road in a series of convoys to Banja Luka and Belgrade, soldiers still
in uniform walking barefoot, farmers pulling their families in tractors, war profiteers whizzing by in green Mercedes—an entire
(failed) "state on the road," as one refugee remarked. As of this writing, this was the largest single wave of refugees of the war. The first
major wave of refugees began three years earlier, in 1992, when the
Yugoslav army and Serbian troops attacked Vukovar and other
cities in eastern Slavonia (the eastern part of Croatia), forcing
thousands of Croatians to flee westward and abroad. In Bosnia-
Herzegovina, waves of refugees also began in 1992 and escalated
over the next three years, as the policy of "ethnic cleansing"[12] forced
entire Muslim communities, and to a lesser extent Croatian and Serbian communities, to flee to other locations in Bosnia-Herzegovina
and abroad, sometimes escaping before the enemy army invaded,
sometimes being shelled, raped, or used as "human shields" on the
road to safety, other times moving from prison camp to life in exile.
Throughout this process, the world community passively watched
or even aided entire populations becoming "uprooted," "ex-

---

mental sources for total figures. Given the difficulty in counting refugees and the
susceptibility of any figures to political manipulation, we warn the reader against
relying on *any* figures.

12. While the term "ethnic cleansing" has been popularized and misused in the
media, people from Muslim, Croatian, and Serbian communities technically are not
of different ethnicities—they are all Slav people. To the extent that a difference
exists, it is one created and imagined by religion, geography, customs, history, and,
to some extent, variances in language. Within ex-Yugoslavia, these groupings were
known as "nations." This use of "nation," however, is often confusing to Westerners
and others accustomed to thinking in terms of "nation states" divided by borders
and different political systems. The nations of ex-Yugoslavia (i.e., Croatian, Muslim,
Serbian) were not neatly grouped within republic boundaries. See *Statistical Year-
book of Yugoslavia* (Belgrade: Federal Bureau of Statistics, 1990).

changed," and "ethnically cleansed"—ugly euphemisms for tearing
people from their homes and destroying cultures and communities.
In July 1995, for example, the international community stood by as
Bosnian Serbs expelled the entire population of Srebrenica, over
40,000 people, many of whom were Muslim refugees from other
locations; thousands of these people are still unaccounted for and
presumed dead.

We have sought to include as many voices from these waves of
refugees as possible. While the majority of authors for this collection
are Bosnian Muslims, reflecting the refugee population, contributors
include ethnic Croats from Bosnia-Herzegovina, Croats from Croatia, ethnic Serbs from Bosnia, and others from Bosnia who, even
now, prefer to identify themselves as only Bosnian or Yugoslav. By
including authors of every ethnic stripe who have fled to every location that would accept them—from Sarajevo to Zagreb, Belgrade
to Islamabad—we emphasize that suffering has no ethnic boundaries. As these stories demonstrate, all groups of civilians in this war,
to different degrees and at different times, have been used by their
own leaders, attacked by the enemy, and pushed out of their communities. We do not equalize blame or somehow excuse the Serbian
nationalist agenda which began and fanned the flames of war and
the Croatian nationalist policies which conspired in this process, or
condone the human rights violations by any group or individual (including refugees themselves). Nor do we imply that all of the authors necessarily share the same vision of the past and future or that
all of them have suffered in an identical manner. To be sure, the
lives of refugees are better when they are closer to their old way of
life and when they can benefit from the support of family, friends,
and others who have the means and willingness to respond. And
their problems are much worse when they must also cope with scars
from a concentration camp, wounds from the front line, and the loss
of loved ones. But it is not the purpose of this book to judge whose
case is worse and whose case is better. All refugees, *as refugees,* have
their own stories to tell.

The Voices of Women Refugees

The vast majority of the authors are women since, as in nearly every refugee population, over 80 percent of the refugees from Bosnia-Herzegovina and Croatia are women and children. Humanitarian aid and human rights groups alike tend to forget this fact, still picturing the model refugee as male. Perhaps this explains why most aid packages exclude sanitary pads and other materials directly related to women's needs; these supplies are distributed separately as if they are for special cases. And perhaps this explains why human rights groups tend to focus most on what happens to men in conflict; the ordeal of the women left fleeing with the children is quietly erased, silenced, forgotten.

Women are rarely seen as women in situations of conflict or in places of refuge. Women may be counted as Palestinians, Rwandans, Bosnians, but rarely as women. Violation of women's human rights and dignity is often viewed as too specific to women to be "human rights" or too generic to human beings to be "women's rights." Yet, although women in war and in refuge are violated in many ways in which men are violated, they are also violated in ways men are not, and these violations do in fact raise serious human rights questions. Women have their own stories to tell—both as victims of a particular group and as women.

Soldiers use rape and other forms of sexual violence to break women and to humiliate them and their men. While men also experience rape and sexual violence in conflict situations, women are targeted in particular. Rape and sexual violence in conflict situations may be part of a planned strategy to terrorize a population, a strategy to use women to satisfy the sexual wants of soldiers as well as acts of individual soldiers that are not necessarily preplanned (though they are often condoned by superiors). In addition, when women are tortured in interrogation and imprisonment, the torture may be of a particular sexual nature. While the women authors here rarely speak of the abuses that have gone before, especially because that was not the focus of our inquiry, the reader should remember that many women refugees are survivors of these forms of sexual violence and torture.

Despite the far-reaching consequences of conflict upon women, their voices are silenced in all levels of decision making about war, from the UN Security Council to international peacekeeping forces. While women throughout the region have organized refugee support groups for themselves and although many women have been on the forefront of antimilitarism and peace groups, women are rarely included in official government efforts to resolve conflicts. Women are routinely excluded from the aftermath of armed conflict, including peace negotiations, peacekeeping monitors, war crimes tribunals, and the highest levels of decision making about humanitarian aid.

Here, however, women refugees have a voice.

These women are not angels of their homes. They don't even have a home. Some of them even thought of killing the angel in them in order to be free, to live better, to remember, to write. But today on the roads of the world, the angel in them lives as a ghost who will once again thrust upon their shoulders the burden of history, the tradition of women's responsibility for survival, the maintenance of life, and the thin thread of common sense. Civilization's progress in the twentieth century has betrayed them as did Titania's love potion: victims of rape, torture, genocide, starvation, the brutality of watching their children and loved ones killed and tortured, and other acts of physical and mental war violence. Together with their children, these women have been simultaneously cast out of history and made guardians of all that has come before.

None of these women *wanted* to tell their stories. Few of them thought anyone would care to hear about their lives as refugees. But all of them knew that they would write a different story than the official version, that they would tell the "little stories" of real life as a refugee. When they realized that they could write and that they would be taken seriously, some of them even wanted to sign their names.

The "small talk" of women belongs to those songs which make life more bearable, the lullabies which comfort us that everything will eventually pass, the bad we are enduring now, the good we have lost. Women's words are the substance which qualifies victory or defeat, the wisdom which challenges the slaughter, the power of the powerless which demands to be heard.

Women refugees write differently than other authors about war: they use details from their everyday lives to tell us about the killing of the most visible life during times of peace—everyday life. They trust emotions, common sense, and that common denominator of humanity, "Don't kill." Their words push us as waves of some enormous sea which may one day wash over everything and set things straight in this world. Even when victimized by war games, political power plays, and the media, the dignity of women refugees isn't lost but only attacked; their cry isn't vindictive but silent; their reasoning and writing, usually invisible, only become sharper and clearer. "And if one person hears and understands a little better," as one woman author said, "it will be worth the pain."

ORGANIZING THE SUITCASE

Nearly all refugees swear that "we didn't believe it could happen to us." But everything that happened could happen to all of us. In the first chapter of this collection, "The Journey Out," refugees from Bosnia-Herzegovina and Croatia speak of the incredible trauma of leaving home and the risks they took. They stuffed photographs, rocks from their gardens, chocolate bars, and their children's underpants into a suitcase and crawled through the woods on their bellies, drove stolen cars through combat zones, paid their last German marks to a UN soldier, hopped on a bus, a plane, a Red Cross ship, an armored carrier . . . and got out.

Once free from the immediate menace of shelling and sniper fire, refugees have time to relive memories of those left behind, of walks in the town square that no longer exists, of drinking coffee in a living room that is now occupied by another family who used to be called neighbor and friend. For readers from countries and areas that have already lost their sense of community (and in particular many Americans), the deep attachment to place in "Dreams of Home" may be utterly foreign. The people of Croatia and Bosnia-Herzegovina pass around worn postcards of their towns and build toy models of their streets so their children will never forget. On the other hand, those who stayed behind lose their dreams of their past lives when everything changes before their eyes (with and without their willing participation). So the refugees are the keepers of the dream of home.

The chapter "Everyday Refugee Life" is organized around waiting. "One thing I've learned from all this," one Bosnian refugee in Pakistan explained, "is how to steal days from God. Every day I pray that it is night and every night I pray that it is day." Time for refugees spells danger; it forces them to remember, and at the same time it threatens to take them far from themselves, stripping them of who they once were and what they once desired. Refugees must fight for control over even the most basic elements of human life. College professors and farmers crowded into a gymnasium eat peaches when given peaches, bathe when someone turns the hose on in the yard, sleep on the same gray mats when the lights are turned off. They struggle to prepare birthday surprises for their children, stand in long lines for visas and humanitarian aid, weave handicrafts for sale through local women's groups, and hang photos of home on their refugee camp walls. But mostly the refugees, no matter where they are, wait for the time they can return home.

Refugee children never stop dreaming, even though they know too much to believe in make-believe anymore. In the chapter entitled "Children's Voices," a ten-year-old girl has nightmares about the time soldiers shot her mother, and, in her sleep, she sees her mother in heaven. A three-year-old boy dreams of an airplane to take him home—the only plane he had ever been on was the one that brought him away from Bosnia. A thirteen-year-old girl dreams of a "room of her own," and an eleven-year-old girl wants only to eat lunch with her mother in her kitchen. In many refugee families, the children speak the best English, so they quickly assume adult roles, filling out visa forms, negotiating with foreign humanitarian aid groups, coaxing their mothers to "please stop crying and study your English."

Many refugees have given up all hope of returning home. Sobered by months and even years in cramped quarters in refugee camps or private accommodations, they realize that the multiethnic society in which they used to live no longer exists. The final chapter, "Starting Life Anew," tells the stories of the refugees who have turned from the process of waiting. They move to Zagreb, St. Louis, Nuremberg, any place that will open its doors. They enroll in language classes, pack their kids off to new schools, accept menial jobs despite their advanced education, volunteer at local women's refugee groups, and start over, never forgetting all they've left behind.

We have organized the stories into these five categories. Sometimes the fit is perfect. Sometimes it is a tight squeeze and even a random selection as many stories span several categories. And all deserve to be published alone. We print the stories with only a brief introduction at the beginning of each chapter, reserving commentary for the afterwords, where Dubravka Ugresic, Marieme Helie-Lucas, and Judith Mayotte all force us to think beyond the Balkans, to listen to the wisdom of refugees, and to support efforts for building long-lasting tolerance and peace.

This book was completed in August 1995, but the voices of refugees are not bound by any fixed date. They need to be heard yesterday, today, and tomorrow. As this book goes to press the war has ended, but few refugees have managed to return home. Through these words, the editors and contributors hope that the world community will begin to understand the magnitude of its responsibility to refugees as human beings in long-term crisis. After all, we all could be refugees.

Julie Mertus and Jasmina Tesanovic
New York and Belgrade, August 1995

*"I shook the hand of my
neighbor when I left. We
had grown up together. I
think he took my house."*

*"We watched the television,
but we never thought it
could happen to us."*

*"I left and he stayed. From
the second we parted, a
pain opened inside me, so
large that it will never
heal."*

Most of these refugees didn't have a choice of whether or not to stay behind. They were physically thrown out of their homes, put into concentration camps, or at best they found some way to leave before soldiers or paramilitary troops invaded their towns, raping, stealing, destroying, killing. They traveled on buses, in cars, in UNHCR and other humanitarian aid trucks (with or without paying a fee), on boats, on foot, with or without documents, photographs, suitcases, plastic bags overflowing with belongings—leaving behind family members, older relatives who refused to budge, younger men who stayed to fight, aunts and uncles who could not be found, young people who refused to get on the truck at the last moment. Some of them knew where they were headed, but most knew only that they were going "out," wherever that was, to "some place safe." They left a month's supply of cat food on the floor for their pets, their laundry hanging in the yard, their jewelry buried underneath a wooden fence, their winter preserves carefully stored in the cellar; they all knew that they would be back "soon."

Many refugees were helped by neighbors, often those very people who were now supposed to be enemies. As one Muslim woman said, "I don't know if those were friends or not who helped us out of Bosnia, who gave us papers for foreign countries. True friends would have helped us stay in our homes, alive. But for us it was a question of life or death, so we had to consider them as friends." Many regret not staying behind, not standing beside loved ones, not dying at one's own home. An old woman who made it to Austria lamented, "I am looking for a place to die, but there is no such place for me. I think my soul will be wandering in eternity, just like my heart is suffering now."

These voices are very painful to hear. They ring of ancient tragedy and eternal truth. They are simple and straightforward. In some cases, the words themselves can add nothing to the bare facts they state. Yet these stories are not simply documents of facts. No matter what cruelty they bespeak, the voices maintain their own dignity, remembering a separation from all that once was believable, a journey into the unknown.

Woman, 41 years old, and her daughter, 18 years old, Sarajevo

MY DAUGHTER'S EYES: A MOTHER/DAUGHTER STORY

MOTHER: I know too much now. The best thing is that we're now all together. I don't know where to start.

DAUGHTER: We all knew that war was coming. My father was in Libya working to support the high cost of my younger brother's expensive medical care for his chronic illness. So my mother was taking care of all of us—me and my three brothers and sisters. One day, Mother came in and said, "Kids, wake up! We must go now." I helped gather my brothers and sisters and we all went down into the basement.

MOTHER: We spent two and a half months in that basement. There were over fifty people in my basement.

DAUGHTER: She tried to move us somewhere else, where there would be more room, but there was no place to go. I was the biggest problem for my mother. She was afraid that I would be raped.

MOTHER: I knew that somehow I had to get my children out of there. One day, I found two cars that worked and I found some gas. Then,

I saw a Serb on the street. He was about thirty years old and he had a long scar on his face—he was pretty ordinary looking. I had never seen him before and I didn't even know his name, but he had a good face, a kind face. I approached him and asked for help. He said, "Come tomorrow and pack your things."

DAUGHTER: The next day, we went to this man with my brothers and sisters. He was waiting in the car. All of us kids got in, but Mother had to stay behind because there wasn't any room. . . .

We were all crying, but when we passed by the Serb soldiers, we had to pretend that we were happy. We had to sit and wave at them like we were going on a holiday. That was the hardest part. The man drove the car through the sector controlled by Serbs. We went about twelve kilometers and then we were at the edge of the Croatian side. The man stopped the car and said, "Get out. I can't go any further." As soon as we got out of the car with our bags, soldiers appeared out of nowhere. We were afraid but they helped us. We went to the house of a friend we knew there. He brought us to the "children's embassy," where they gave us food and then said, "Go alone."

I used all of the money my mother had given me to buy tickets for all of us to Croatia. The bus ride was a nightmare—twenty-four hours and thirty people on a small bus. First we went to Split, then Makarska, then Promajna. That first month, we had nothing. Just one room and three beds for six people. We didn't even have sheets. As the oldest, I tried to take care of everyone. I didn't hear anything about my mother.

After a month, I met a Croatian soldier who said he would take a letter to my mother. A cousin got the letter and contacted me. He kept saying that everything was OK, but I felt that everything wasn't OK. He couldn't say anything precise about Mother. When I finally heard that she really was OK, I was so happy that I danced in the streets. My heels were broken on my shoes, but I kept dancing. I was so happy, but somehow, I still couldn't believe it. I wanted everything to be fine, but without hearing my mother's voice, I couldn't believe anything.

MOTHER: I kept a phone in the fireplace of my house, so that I could make calls and no one would hear. When my daughter got to the Croatian side, she called to say that she was OK, and our Croat friends called to say that they had left for Croatia. But then nothing. I kept the phone in the fireplace but I didn't hear anything after that.

DAUGHTER: My mother saved at least forty people. She found food for everyone when there was no food. She wore a very big skirt. Whenever people came into the basement in our house, she would make them give her their guns, and she would hide them in her skirt. Then, she would take them from her skirt and bury them in the yard. So there would be no weapons in the house if soldiers came. . . .

The Serbs came and caught her brother and brother-in-law and put them in prison. And then she stopped helping other people. Then she just tried to get them out of prison. You could pay the Serbs and they would bring food to the prison.

MOTHER: Over 480 men on our street were captured; until this day, we haven't heard from 130 of them. After the men were rounded up, they started gathering up the women. One Serb friend came to my house and said, "You must go to an interview."

DAUGHTER: I knew him, too; he was my classmate from high school.

MOTHER: They put me in a prison in a basement. There were ten women in one room—two were older women, and the rest were between the ages of thirty and forty.

DAUGHTER: This is the first time I'm hearing this!

MOTHER: From then on, every day was the same. We had one meal a day and we had one chance to go to the bathroom a day, and we were never allowed to shower. They gave us nothing for menstruation. The women who were bleeding would sit in a corner. Like animals . . . there was nothing else we could do.

There was no light in the basement so we all sat in darkness. And it was so cold, we all began to get sick. They would put smoke bombs in the prison just to scare us and they would eat in front of us, just to tease us. But, maybe because one of the prisoners was married to a Serb, they didn't do anything really bad to us. . . .

I kept thinking that at least my children were in a better place. I wasn't sure where they were, but I knew it was better. . . .

After two months in the basement like that, I was saved. The Serb who had helped my children came in the middle of the night and stole me from the prison. He threw me in the trunk of a car and drove me off. I still don't even know his name. . . .

I don't know why he helped me. Maybe it was because they all knew that my husband wasn't a soldier.

DAUGHTER: What did you do?

MOTHER: I hid in the trunk of my car by our house. There was shooting all around. Another neighbor gave me petrol. I got in the front seat of my car and waited, but the shooting didn't stop. I was sitting, slouched in the seat with men on one side of me shooting at men on the other. There was a Serb soldier's car right in front of me. He started driving and I began following him. I just kept driving until I was on the other side [the Croatian side]. Now, when I think about it, I must have been crazy; but I wasn't thinking. I was like a crazy one.

When I got to the other side, I went to my Croatian friend's house, and I waited until nightfall.

DAUGHTER: She was ashamed. She didn't want our friend to see her in the light—she had been wearing the same clothes for two months and she had never had a shower.

MOTHER: I had a bad fever. As soon as I rang our friend's doorbell and he opened the door, I fainted.

DAUGHTER: She had pneumonia and arthritis and who knows what else.

MOTHER: I stayed for five days, but I couldn't wait any longer. My friend gave me some money and some clothes. I still had a fever when I got in my car again and drove to Croatia. . . .

I was alone. I kept fighting off hitchhiking paramilitary groups who wanted a ride. It was too dangerous to have anyone in the car with me. I had to fight to be alone.

DAUGHTER: Our friend called me to say that my mother was coming. I almost died with joy. But when, after two days, she didn't arrive, I began to think he was lying.

MOTHER: It took a long time because I could only travel at night and the car was very slow.

DAUGHTER: But she came! When I first saw her, I didn't recognize her because she looked so bad. We started weeping and holding each other. We both thought, "We must find Dad."

MOTHER: He didn't have a passport, but even without one, he crossed into nine countries, weaving his way to Croatia. He went to Malta, Turkey, Italy, Germany, Austria, and who knows where else, on his way to Croatia.

DAUGHTER: When my father called from Zagreb, the first thing my mother said was, "Where are you?" Then she started to cry. She didn't even ask, "How are you?" Just, "Where are you?"

MOTHER: He came down to Promajna but stayed for only two weeks. Then, he put on a soldier's uniform and went back to Bosnia to buy all of our family members' freedom. He used all of the money he had made in Libya to bring everyone out. He got stuck in Croatia when they closed the border. Then, two months later, they sent us all to Pakistan.

DAUGHTER: We're trying to get to Canada, but we're too sick. Our family can't pass the physicals necessary for entry. My mother is still sick from the prison. Four months ago, she had a heart attack and now she has bad kidney problems. And my brother has his chronic illness, and at least another one of us is very sick whenever we try to test healthy.

MOTHER: We're waiting. . . .

How did I sustain myself through all this? When I closed my eyes,

I just thought of my daughter's eyes. She has such lovely, large brown eyes. Doesn't she? Everything is OK because we're alive.

Islamabad, Pakistan, August 1994

The mother and daughter are two of over four hundred Bosnian refugees who ended up in Pakistan. Originally, they sought refuge along the Croatian coast. When fighting between Muslims and Croats escalated in the spring of 1993, Croatia gave them forty-eight hours to leave. Pakistan, honoring some sense of solidarity with other Muslim communities, offered a haven. Enticed by rumors of swimming pools and bungalows, the Bosnians agreed, under-standing that their stay in Pakistan would be a short one en route to a more appropriate location. Neither the Bosnians nor the Pakistani officials got what they expected. Dressed in short shorts and T-shirts, the secular Bosni-ans could not fit into the traditional, Islamic Pakistan. While the Pakistanis tried to offer their best hospitality, they could not change the sweltering hot weather or their culture. They tucked the Bosnians away in the Hajji com-plex — dormitories built for migrating pilgrims. Without any chance or desire to assimilate into their new surroundings, the Bosnians stayed confined to their concrete-block rooms, waiting for a chance to leave.

The mother decided to tell her story only after Julie Mertus and Eve Ensler (a screenplay writer) had spent over two weeks listening to refugee stories in the Hajji complex. Sitting on the floor with her knees pulled up to her chest and her back pressed against the wall, she called her daughter over to help her . . . and she began to speak. Her daughter had never heard the story before.

After a year and a half in Pakistan, the family finally reached Canada at the end of 1994. They still dream of returning home.

Woman, 38 years old, Teslic

THE NEIGHBOR

We stayed the first two years from the beginning of the war. We lived in fear but nobody touched us at first. I was alone in the house; my husband is an Albanian who works in Macedonia. We were very afraid that if some of their people got killed, they would no longer say hello to us, as if we were the ones who did it. Then our neighbors started to disturb us. It was our neighbors, not the refugees who came into our village. I won't blame those who are not guilty.

I came to this Hungarian camp a year ago, not knowing what would happen next. I came with my children of nineteen and seven years old. I took only a few things with me. We had to have one thousand German marks per person and another five hundred marks to pay to the municipal authorities. You have to have a thousand papers in order to get out.

My cousin was killed in his home, that is why we left. A neighbor killed him in the middle of the night, because his brother was killed on the front line. Even though my cousin was a Muslim volunteering in the Serbian army, wounded when fighting for his village. The neighbor just fired bullets into him, without a word. Revenge. The police came and they took the murderer to prison in Banja Luka, but what is the use of it? Three days later, young men between the ages of twenty-five and thirty massacred a man in our village only because his name was Alija.

Before the war we didn't know who was what, we all had our houses next to each other: in my village Serbs and Muslims lived together. My best friend was a Serbian woman, but they cannot protect us now, because now they call us "balije" [a derogatory term for Muslim]. I don't even know what it means.

I had to sell everything at half price to smugglers in order to get money for the trip. And I was happy that somebody wanted to buy it.

They harassed me and another woman in the village. I worked in a neighbor's house and I would stay there to sleep because I was afraid to be alone in my house with the children. I went at dusk to my place with my son just to feed our cow. A man came up to my front door with a mask over his face. He took me by my hand and dragged me outside the house. My son saw it. This man dragged me to the stable. I fought back but he stripped my clothes off. He took me to the back of the house and started to kiss me, saying, "You are a woman, you must give yourself to me." I didn't know yet who he was, I thought he was one of the postmen, but when I took the mask off his face and recognized him as a neighbor I felt even worse, I got more afraid. So often he had sat at our place, drank coffee with us. He had even worked for me.

He raped me. I told nobody because I didn't want to cause panic. Not even my husband. I am afraid of blood revenge. That must not happen. My son saw it, but he also keeps quiet.

This man wanted to come every day and rape me, and he was young enough to be my son; he also was only nineteen. That is why I left, I couldn't defend myself. He could do anything he wanted. We had no rights. Once in the post office they didn't even let me send my husband a letter. Then the postman's wife shouted and they let me do it. The same in the shops: they had known me for years but suddenly they didn't want to speak to me, they just wanted me out of the way.

But listen to this true story from my village: A Serb, a very rich man, gave a lot of money for the Serbian army from the very beginning of the war. One day an armed group named Red Caps came to his door; they were robbers, they would take anything from anybody but they called themselves Serbs. When they came to this Serb's house, which was the most beautiful in the village, he took a gun and shouted at the gang leader. The gang left, only to return the next day. The man, his wife, and children had to flee; they burned his whole house. There are other Serbian houses which were robbed; there are no more Muslim houses and now my village is Serbian property.

Camp Bicke, 30 km from Budapest, Hungary, May 1995

As early as December 18, 1992, the UN Security Council condemned mass rapes in Bosnia, finding that Bosnian Serb soldiers in particular had raped Muslim and Croat women, both in detention camps and in individual towns and villages, as part of a strategy to coerce non-Serb residents to leave their homes. Evidence gathered by the United Nations and independent human rights groups indicates that although all sides have committed rape, the bulk of the evidence of "systematic rape" — rape as part of an apparent war strategy to terrorize and eliminate a population — points to Bosnian Serbs raping Muslim and Croatian women. Rape in war, whether deemed systematic or not, can constitute a war crime, a "crime against humanity," or a grave human rights violation under international law. The War Crimes Tribunal for the Former Yugoslavia, established in 1994 (and later expanded to include war crimes in Rwanda and renamed), explicitly includes rape as a prosecutable offense under several provisions of the statute drawn up by the United Nations to guide its course.

Like most women raped in the war, this woman never had any opportunity for counseling or for any medical care for injury caused by the rapes — apart from receiving some heavy sedatives to mute her pain. This is the first time she ever told anyone her story, but she had no problem telling it to Jasmina Tesanovic, a Serb from Belgrade. Jasmina remembers: "Eventually she gave me lunch I couldn't refuse, this wonderful gibanica *(pie) she managed to bake in the camp, and she said, 'Eat it, you will not regret eating one of the last Bosnian pies I am making.' Eating with refugees I spoke to became a sacred ritual. It was my only way to pay them back for their hospitality. This happened everywhere in Europe and the United States. Our meal represented a statement of our intimacy and mutual trust. Once they even offered me shoes for my young daughter since I lived in Belgrade under sanctions." (Sanctions did not have such a harsh impact on most residents of reduced Yugoslavia — provided they had money to pay for smuggled goods.)*

Nizima, 38 years old, Janja

I AM NOT A BALIJA

I was a tailor. I lived in Janja, which is now occupied by Serbs. I had a boutique and my husband was a folk singer. Now he washes dishes. We had everything but we were very simple people. My husband doesn't want to sing here. He is in solidarity with people in Bosnia; when he sings here, everybody starts to cry.

When Bijeljina fell and Arkan came in with his special troops and massacred civilians, people just disappeared. All those who had at least something . . . whole families would just disappear. Simply disappear. We didn't feel safe anymore, so we decided to leave everything. I came to Vienna with a paper bag for a suitcase in 1992.

The first time I tried to get out was with my sister and her two girls. My husband stayed behind because we were afraid that he might be caught and sent to the concentration camp for Muslims in Batkovici like many were. But at the border with Serbia the police said, "You balijas cannot cross the border." There were so many armies, special troops, police that I couldn't tell any difference. All of them stopped the buses and asked stupid things. This guy who entered the bus announced, "All balijas out of the bus." At that time I didn't know what *balija* was. I knew what I was not; I was not a balija, so I sat peacefully. Then he got crazy and made me get out of the bus, cursing me. In front of the bus a drunk man with a long beard and a strange cap, red eyes and a knife stained with blood stood saying, "Is there a balija I have to kill?" As my blood froze in my veins, I remembered the movies about Partisans and Chetniks and I realized that he looked exactly like a Chetnik from the movies.

I saw a policeman standing by, a man I knew, he used to come to the bar where my husband sang and he knew me. At that time the police weren't yet so nationalistic, so I ran up to him and asked him if he could help me get on a bus. He was afraid to help me but he said, "I will put you on a bus and then you will go away from this place. Never come back, you, your sister and the girls!" I realized what was going on. People were taken off the buses and taken to a concentration camp. I looked around me: there was this bridge I could jump off and be killed rather than go to a camp. All the territory around was full of mines so we could not run away; the only escape was the bridge. The girls were trembling with fear looking at the bloody hands of the Chetnik. There were ninety of us altogether. But then a bus came, a policeman stopped it and made us get inside. The bus took us back to Bijeljina. The driver stopped at every village saying, "If I have to drive balijas, I can stop for my people too." Once we reached Bijeljina, I remember those one hundred meters on foot to my mother's house. They lasted an eternity. But still I felt safer in Bijeljina since nobody could tell from your face if you were a balija or not.

However, a week later we tried to leave again. This time we paid a Serb who guaranteed transportation to Vienna for everybody. This man helped many Muslims leave Bosnia safely. He made a lot of money, but he would do it even for free if you had no money. I don't know if it was all arranged, but I think he was a good man. We finally came to Vienna and now when I try to tell my story I still cannot find the right words to express my horror, and my emotions come back. How come we can all live together here and not there in our homes?

When I came here, I had to go to the camp. We had some position in our society, but here you have fallen so low that you have to wait for people to give you soap in order to wash. My husband, who has smoked since he was a kid, cannot live without cigarettes, but he cannot buy them.

Now we work, we do all kinds of jobs to earn money and try to get the rest of our family out of Bosnia. They pay us very little and we work very hard. But I keep quiet and work, I have no choice. If they offend me, I cry only when alone, on the bus or at home. Still now I cry every day, and I have a feeling I will never overcome my loss. I would go back tomorrow if only I could. People there had less than here but still we were more generous and friendly. It is a different mentality; it is difficult for me to live alone here.

We are Muslims, but not from Arabia. Neither my grandmother, my mother nor me ever wore those national clothes for women. We went to the mosque but we were a progressive European people, whatever they say now. It was not possible to have in Bosnia a national Muslim state because we were three nations from the very beginning and that is how it has to stay; no nation can be dominant. Nobody can take me back in history and make me cover my face and my body; we the Muslims from Bosnia are not that way. And even today in the midst of the war the Bosnian passport bears the symbol of three peoples living together. And we have a Bosnian passport, not a Muslim one.

My father and my mother came here as refugees with a plastic bag, leaving everything behind like me. In order to avoid them seeing me cleaning the toilets in the camp, I fought for this flat and a different job. In the camp I cleaned toilets without being paid on all three religious holidays, Muslim, Catholic and Orthodox, to make a point. And some people would make all kinds of mess on purpose, but I would just clean up again. I know all religious holidays and respect them all because that was how we used to live. After cleaning the toilets over and over again, I would say a prayer to Allah and ask him finally this: If there is no justice for me in this world, please if he would take me up, up high in the heaven to him.

Vienna, Austria, May 1995

Arkan, the man who this woman says took her town, is Zeljko Raznjatovic, perhaps the most infamous Serbian war criminal. Serb irregulars under Arkan's command have committed scores of wartime atrocities, including rapes and murders of civilians, destruction of religious and cultural landmarks, and brutal treatment of prisoners in detention. According to human rights groups, substantial evidence ties Arkan to the regular Yugoslav army (the JNA, or Yugoslav National Army), which has been largely credited with supplying irregular troops like Arkan's and for masterminding their movements.

Chetniks were elite troops of the Royal Army of the Kingdom of Serbia in World War I. In World War II, Chetniks were troops devoted to the king and known for their brutality and war crimes. Today, the term is used by some Bosnian Serb groups with pride to describe themselves and by others as a derogatory term for all Serbs. Partisans were members of the People's Liberation Army led by the Communist Party in World War II.

Nizima's story is a common one. After nearby towns fell to gangs of irregular soldiers, Nizima did not wait to see what would happen to her own home, fleeing immediately for safety. By the time Serbian forces reached Nizima's town, few non-Serbian residents remained. Terror was an effective aid in so-called "ethnic cleansing" — the process of pushing all people of another ethnonational group out of an area. In Nizima's town, Serb refugees from other parts of Bosnia-Herzegovina took the homes that the Muslims had left behind. In other parts of the war-torn country, Muslims or Croats took the homes of Serbs as they fled to safer ground. By 1995, an estimated two-thirds of the residents of Bosnia-Herzegovina had been "displaced" — sometimes more than once.

Nizima told her story on a Sunday — "the worst day of the week," she said, "because on this day we realize most we are away from home."

Gordana Ibrovic, 41 years old, Sarajevo

THE MOST BEAUTIFUL CITY IN THE WORLD, GOOD-BYE

For the first few months of the war, I never even contemplated leaving Sarajevo. I kept thinking the war would end and we would rebuild the city. But the months went by, there was less and less food, it was getting colder, and Pofalici, a precarious part of town, had been without water since the beginning of the war. One of the reasons I wanted to leave was because of my son Dario. Like the other children, he didn't realize the dangers posed by the shells. He kept going outside, and our area was a place where lots of people were killed or wounded. My daughter Lana listened to us and spent the whole time indoors.

We thought that if we left Sarajevo we would be back by spring at the latest, and both Safet and I felt we should take the children away. Had I known I'd be away this long, I'd never have left Sarajevo. Since I didn't return in the spring of 1993 as I had thought, I've stopped thinking about any particular spring at all. But I know that one day I'll go back.

Safet wanted us to leave, but every time there was a convoy he'd change his mind. Our kids were big. Lana was eleven; we were afraid of rape. Dario was fifteen and, big as he was, he could have had a rifle shoved into his hands somewhere along the way. We left on November 16, 1992. We heard on the radio that the HVO [Croatian military defense] was taking Croats from Stup to Kiseljak. We got a place on the bus because my husband passed one hundred German marks to one of the organizers. Ten buses left Sarajevo that day.

In Kiseljak we spent the night with a Croatian friend of my husband's. He suggested that we proceed immediately to Split because it might start to snow. We reached Gruda and the Croatian border without problems. Although we had a letter of guarantee for Split, the Croatian police kicked all three of us off the bus, without a word of explanation and for reasons I'll never know. Meanwhile, there were people entering Croatia without any papers whatsoever. We did not manage to enter Croatia. Finally we were taken to a school in Siroki Brijeg, where refugees from Jajce were housed. All they gave us were blankets and mats. It was a very cold night. I thought to myself: Why on earth did I ever leave home?

The next day, November 18, 1992, my relative in Split found two Croatian women who came for the children and me in two separate cars with Croatian license plates. They drove us into Croatia without any problem. We went in one car and the luggage went in another. That was a precaution in case we were stopped by the police. I offered to pay the two women, but they wouldn't accept any money. They said they simply wanted to help. And so we spent the next twelve days with relatives in Split. I listened to the news; there was talk of renewed war in Croatia after the new year. I didn't want to stay there with the children. Since we were staying with relatives in Split, we hadn't registered as refugees. We bought plane tickets for Istanbul and left on November 29, 1992, to stay with my husband's relatives there. We spent eight months in Turkey, until July 10, 1993.

I found those eight months in Istanbul harder than all our eight months in besieged Sarajevo. Their mentality and way of life are completely different from ours in Bosnia, and we found it hard to adjust. The children were safe, which was the main thing. During this time I discovered that Bosnian Muslims, in terms of their way of life and customs, lean towards the West, not the East. We didn't register as refugees in Turkey because we were staying with close relatives, with my mother-in-law's sister and her children, but we couldn't stand it there. They didn't understand the situation in Sarajevo. They didn't understand that we stayed with them so long not because we wanted to, but because we had to, because we had nowhere else to go.

We had arrived in Turkey without any money, except for fifty German marks given to us by one relative. None of our other relatives gave or offered a cent. Still, we were never without money because all three of us worked nonstop. We did all sorts of jobs: first we worked in a sportswear factory, then in a ready-made clothes factory, then in a shoe shop. Our working hours were from eight in the morning until eight or nine at night.

We were out of the house all day long; we only came back to sleep. All the same, we became a burden to the whole family; they didn't want to keep us any longer. They told us quite openly to go, and when we asked where would we go, they said they didn't know. Moving to a refugee camp somewhere in Turkey was out of the question because I heard, and once even saw, that camp conditions were bad. I shuddered at the thought of life in the camp, and I was afraid. Had we not had relatives abroad, I never would have left Sarajevo in the first place. I started thinking about going to some other country, because there was obviously nothing for us in Turkey. But many countries had already closed their borders to refugees from Bosnia-Herzegovina. The Czech Republic was one of the few that didn't require visas or letters of guarantee, and my husband had an aunt in Prague. [Entry requirements have become more stringent since the events related here.] She was a refugee but at least she had an apartment. We corresponded with her. She told us we could come and stay with her.

We told our relatives in Turkey that we wanted to move to Prague and, without a word, they counted out four thousand German marks for the plane tickets! Since we weren't registered in Turkey as refugees and we didn't have the necessary papers from the police, we were stopped from boarding the plane in July. Our luggage went on to Prague. After all sorts of problems, we finally left Turkey three days later.

We liked Prague from the very beginning; it reminded us a lot of Sarajevo. But we noticed that my husband's aunt was not all that happy to see us. Despite her earlier promises, she told us the day we arrived that we would have to move.

Ten days after our arrival in Prague, I found a job for myself and my son in a supermarket, marking prices, shelving goods, basically working as helpers. Had we stayed in the aunt's flat, our earnings would have been enough for the three of us but the situation in the house was becoming unbearable. My husband's aunt kept making scenes, saying we had to find a place of our own.

We stayed in our new flat only a month. Our earnings at the supermarket weren't enough to cover the rent, utilities and food, and my working hours didn't let me take on an extra job. That entire period was like a living nightmare. I would buy the papers, read the want ads, phone around and scour the city, looking for another, higher-paid, job. For the first time in my life, I didn't sleep for nights on end. That hadn't happened to me even in besieged Sarajevo during the worst of the shelling. The next month's rent was soon due. I found a job in a bakery, where I could earn 420 German marks a month. But even that wasn't enough. We had to find a cheaper flat and we simply didn't have the time to do it. We wound up out on the street.

Winter was approaching and I was already quite exhausted. Everyone advised me to go to a refugee camp and recuperate there. I tried as long as I could to make some sort of normal life for all three of us. Suddenly I felt as though I had come up against the wall—I couldn't go on anymore. And so at the tail end of summer, we found ourselves at the Red Cross refugee camp. We arrived on September 9, 1993. We spent twelve days in quarantine there, then two days in Stebno and on September 23 we arrived in Doksy. I hadn't spoken to my husband from mid-June until the end of September. He was going out of his mind in Sarajevo because he didn't know where or how we were. It wasn't until I got here that I started recovering. I realized how exhausted I was from my ten-month struggle to survive. Twenty days later, when I went back to Prague for the first time, people were surprised that I had managed to recuperate in such a short time.

I don't know when I'll return to Sarajevo. All I know is that if my city is completely destroyed, I'll still go back and help rebuild it because to me it is the most beautiful city in the world. I can hardly wait to go back.

Prague, The Czech Republic, 1995

Bosnians voted for independence in a two-day referendum on February 29, 1992. While most Bosnian Serbs (32 percent of Bosnia's population at the time) boycotted the referendum, overall 63 percent of all eligible Bosnians cast ballots; 99.4 percent of them chose independence. Almost immediately after the vote, fighting began in Sarajevo. Radio Free Europe reported that on March 1 the first shots were fired in Sarajevo. The European Community and the United States recognized Bosnian independence on April 7 (the United States also recognized the independence of Croatia and Slovenia on the same day). Even before the final recognition, Serb troops intensified their shelling of Sarajevo — the siege of Sarajevo began on April 5.

Gordana and her family left Sarajevo on Red Cross buses with over 1,500 Muslims and Croats who were given permission to leave on November 16, 1992, after extensive negotiations. Her transport was supposed to be free. Ironically, on the day Gordana left Sarajevo, UN Secretary General Boutros Boutros-Ghali was instructed to conduct a study on the establishment of safe havens for refugees, thus beginning the UN debate over ways to keep Bosnian refugees safe within their own country.

Like nearly all men, Gordana's husband stayed behind. Men either were not allowed on humanitarian transports unless they were elderly or wounded, or they stayed back to fight. Most able-bodied men who managed to leave paid large bribes for their escape.

Thirteen days before Gordana left Sarajevo, the Serb capture of Jajce forced 35,000 Bosnian Muslims out of their homes. When she listened to this news on the radio, Gordana never dreamed that she would soon be sleeping next to the refugees from Jajce in a schoolhouse. While most refugees from Jajce remained within Bosnia, Gordana's family was relatively privileged because it had enough money to pay for the plane tickets and bribes necessary to get out.

Woman, 58 years old, Bijeljina

AGENCY

My children had all left for Germany, but I stayed alone with my husband because he was sick. They came to throw me out of my house. My husband died the next day; we buried him, but I stayed on because of my mother and my brother. We stayed for two years and by then we couldn't get out anymore.

Thankfully there is an agency in the center of our city of Bijeljina. A man named Dragas runs it, a man from outside, a man from nowhere. He just showed up and set up business. You have to go there and pay by selling your house, of course at a very unfair, low price. You sign that you are leaving everything of your own free will to the state, and then you can get out. The price per person is now five thousand German marks. Otherwise, you cannot get out of the city. Officially it is not permitted. I don't know if it is all arranged, but it is a good thing that there is such an agency. At least one can leave safely. Everyone knows about the agency. Of course we had to use it too.

We paid the agency and then we had to pay an extra one hundred marks to cross the border. At the Hungarian border we gave another four hundred marks to I don't even know whom, and then we spent ten days in quarantine, and now we are here ready to leave for Germany. My sister sent us the letter of guarantee for the visa.

Our life in Bosnia had become impossible. There was a certain man named Vojkan who took men away during the night, to Majevica to work, and women and children were taken to Tuzla. We were afraid and that is why we left, all together: Mother, who is eighty, myself and my brother with his wife. The local Serbs were OK, but they dared not protect us. The ones from outside who came from nowhere, from places I never heard of, they were terrible. They came to take away even my brother, who was a soldier of the Yugoslav regular army. They surrounded my house and we escaped through the back door.

It would take me five days to tell you what it is like in Bijeljina: in Janja and Bijeljina there are no more old Muslims. They would just come to get you during the night and you would disappear. We had to leave because we decided not to fight on any side. What for? Whom for? That is why we decided to go to Germany, not to Turkey where we would be engaged on the other side. We left our rich and beautiful house to a man, a refugee, a wonderful man, a Serb who will take care of it.

When we left, a Serbian woman came to see us off. She was my best friend and we had lived thirty-seven years together. She brought me oranges and tomatoes for the trip. My elderly mother was completely lost and I was desperate.

Budapest, Hungary, May 1995

Serbian forces pushed nearly all of the Muslim residents out of Bijeljina by the end of 1993. Only the older residents, such as this woman, remained behind. When she told this story, she was living in a hotel room on the outskirts of Budapest. Three Muslim families sat together in one room, playing cards and drinking coffee. They were very eager to tell their stories to anyone, even the visiting Serbs from Belgrade. "We all lost our country," this woman said, inviting the Serbian visitors to sit and cry together with her, even as Bosnian Serbs continued to hold some of her relatives captive back home.

Group of women, late 20s to late 30s, Bosnia-Herzegovina
THE PRICE OF PASSAGE

WOMAN 1: How much is it now? I keep hearing different things.

WOMAN 2: I heard it was up to eight thousand German marks in some places.

WOMAN 3: That's impossible! I think four thousand is more like it.

WOMAN 2: Well, your husband might have paid four thousand, but that was a while ago.

WOMAN 4: I heard of someone who paid five thousand last week. He had to wait for a long time but he's out.

WOMAN 3: From Sarajevo?

WOMAN 4: Yeah.

WOMAN 2: All the way out?

WOMAN 4: Yeah.

WOMAN 2: I think it's more.

WOMAN 1: My son said he paid UNPROFOR five thousand [German marks] and they put him in an armored vehicle.

WOMAN 4: Yeah, sounds right.

(Name of country withheld by request), 1994

UNPROFOR—the UN Protection Force—was sent into Croatia and Bosnia-Herzegovina by the UN Security Council to "create the conditions of peace and security required for the negotiation of an overall settlement of the Yugoslav crisis." UNPROFOR began its mission tentatively after the UN Security Council voted on February 21, 1992, to send nearly 14,000 peacekeepers to monitor the cease fire and protect the rights of civilians in fourteen minority enclaves in Croatia (Resolution 743). UNPROFOR's mission then expanded into Bosnia through a series of subsequent UN Security Council resolutions; UNPROFOR troops succeeded in reopening the airport in Sarajevo in June 1992, and in September the UN Security Coun-

*cil authorized an increase in the size of UNPROFOR to protect humanitar-
ian activities in Bosnia. Still, China successfully opposed a U.S.–sponsored
clause that would have allowed the UN troops to use force.*

*As war atrocities spread, UNPROFOR watched on as an awkward by-
stander, its actions criticized by all sides. The UN troops came under harsh-
est attack in the summer of 1995, after they failed to do anything to prevent
Bosnian Serbs from taking Srebrenica, a city designated a safe haven and
the home to 40,000 Muslim refugees. In August 1995, independent presses
in Belgrade reported that thousands of Muslim men had been massacred in
the takeover, but the U.S. press did not report the existence of mass graves
near Srebrenica until two months later.*

*This conversation was overheard by one of the editors attending a women's
refugee support group.*

Aida, 34 years old, Sarajevo

A SUITCASE FOR "GOD HELP ME"

I was a doctor in the emergency room of the JNA Military Hospital
in Sarajevo. While I was at work, wives of Serbian officers came into
the hospital. They told me awful stories and I knew immediately
that even Sarajevo was going to be bombed. I would release soldiers
from their duty, declaring them incapable of fighting because they
would cry because they didn't want to go to the front. That is why I
was placed on the list for liquidation. A military commission put me
on that list in 1992. Special troops from Nis [one of JNA's headquarters in Serbia] came on their way back from Vukovar to take over
the hospital. They went on the roof and shot the sick people we had
been treating. Because I knew that I could be jailed, I took my children and on April 6 went to the military airport with the wives of
military officers, all Serbian. I was the only Muslim. We all left for
Belgrade.

I didn't know anybody in Belgrade. I spent the night in the house of a friend's friend. The next day I took a train for Vienna and left the country for good. I didn't dare go to Croatia because I had been in military service with the JNA. I was a refugee in Slovenia for a year. It was nice; I worked. I hoped I would go back to Sarajevo; that is why I stayed so near. But the war went on, and my husband was held hostage for three days so he had to go to Istanbul. I went with him. It was nice there too; we both worked, but I left Turkey because of the children's education. Since we are Muslims, we got our papers easily for the U.S.A. We have been here six months and I no longer count on going back anymore. But listen to my story, how I ran away.

That day I was taking a walk in Sarajevo; it was a lovely spring day, and I bought the annual ticket for the theater because I am an optimist by nature. But the same day I packed a suitcase for "God help me" and one in case we went to the cellar, full of old things. My girl friends came to have coffee with me. They asked me what I kept under the bed. I said a "God help me" suitcase and a cellar suitcase. We all laughed. When I left a few hours later for the air-port, I mixed up the suitcases and took the one with the old clothes for children. That day was so lovely in Sarajevo, and the irony is that I left for Belgrade with Serbian women running away from the Serbs who persecuted me.

The worst thing for me in this war is the loss of friendships, es-pecially one. I had to bury my friendship toward Ljubinka, who went to Pale. We had been together since we were born, but war erected a wall between us. I don't want to tell her anything; she doesn't want to say anything to me. Those who were once friends cannot be friends anymore. Ljubinka was the one who warned me that the Serbs had decided to fight the war and that we would have to leave. I took her advice, but that is where we finished. I don't understand how she could follow her husband, how she could choose the war.

St. Louis, Mo., U.S.A., April 1995

The JNA was made up of people of all ethnonational backgrounds, so it was not unusual for Aida, a Muslim woman, to be working in the JNA's hospital. However, by the time she fled Sarajevo, most non-Serb generals had been ousted from the JNA, and many lower-ranked, non-Serb soldiers had left on their own accord (often due to coercion or the desire to fight for another side).

Aida mentions JNA soldiers "returning from Vukovar." Vukovar, a city in the eastern part of Croatia known as Eastern Slavonia, was the site of some of the worst destruction in Croatia. On August 25, 1991, the JNA, joined by "irregular," ethnic Serb troops, began a full-scale offensive against Croat defense units and other Croat troops defending Vukovar and the neighboring cities of Osijek and Vinkovci. After an 86-day fight that left over 2,300 people dead and most buildings leveled, Vukovar fell to the Serbs. The JNA then moved from Croatia to Bosnia-Herzegovina. Serb leaders have claimed that the JNA began withdrawing from Sarajevo on May 24, 1992, and that it had removed itself entirely from Bosnia-Herzegovina by November 1992. However, many sources, including many of the refugees who told their stories for this book, have reported seeing JNA soldiers in Bosnia-Herzegovina long after that date.

Aida is one of several Bosnian refugees who are now in St. Louis. She told her story at the Bosnian Club — a new establishment on a deserted street in downtown St. Louis. While the Bosnian Club is frequented mostly by Bosnian Muslims, Croats and Serbs can be found drinking Turkish coffee there too.

Dzemila Kenjar, 20 years old, Kozarac (between Prijedor and Banja Luka)

CRIME AND PUNISHMENT

I was at home that day: May 20, 1992. They ordered us to submit the weapons but we didn't have any. Then they bombed us for three days. We went under the earth; we had nothing to eat. They robbed our houses completely. They found us in the cellar and they separated out the men. They cut the throat of our neighbor. We saw all of that. They took us to the concentration camp through the woods. They put us in a school: there they killed and raped. I was in the concentration camp with my mother, my father, and two brothers. My third brother was in another camp. We were kept by the Serbs, they destroyed our houses, and they wanted me and my cousin for the whorehouse. We managed to run away.

They caught us and took us to Vlasic Mountain, they swore at us and spat at us, and they took us to Travnik where the Bosnian army overtook us. In Travnik we were hungry all the time. We got our papers and we went to Zagreb. In Zagreb we stood in front of a mosque and some people took us to a camp. We stayed there for a year; the most important thing was that it was peaceful. My brother and father stayed in the camp in Bosnia.

We lost everything on our way. They made us throw the things away. We went to Varazdin [in Croatia], then to Karlovac. We got our papers marking us as prisoners from the concentration camp. We had no place to go, we had nothing. We had no luggage. We had had to leave everything in front of the bus so they wouldn't kill us.

Here we have everything. We chose America for the work, so we could work. I think of going back home. Of earning money and going back home. In our country (before the war) no policeman guarded our houses as here in America.

St. Louis, Mo., U.S.A., April 1995

Dzemila, a beautiful young woman with violet eyes, played self-consciously with the baby on her lap as she spoke, glancing occasionally at her mother and father for support. She spoke in short, clipped sentences, refusing to allow herself to remember details. She warned Jasmina Tesanovic, one of the co-editors, that she should leave Belgrade. "I am afraid for you," Dzemila said; "they will get you some time."

Human rights researchers and journalists have reported that Bosnian Serbs raped, murdered, and detained civilians in dozens of northern Bosnian towns and villages — including Dzemila's hometown. The "whorehouse" that Dzemila mentions apparently is one of the "houses" set up in which Muslim girls were repeatedly raped by Serb soldiers. While Dzemila escaped the whorehouse, some of her former classmates did not; she does not know of their fate.

Travnik, the city where Dzemila was held and from where she eventually fled, was the scene of intense fighting between Serbs and Muslims and later, between Muslims and Croats.

Vinka Ljubimir, 32 years old, Dubrovnik

THE PASSAGE

This is not the first time I sit to this—in front of a blank computer screen, deadline ahead of me. And then . . . nothing. Words do not come to me. All I keep thinking is that my story is not anything special, that many other people have lived through worse. For me, a lifetime has passed between the last peaceful summer at home in Dubrovnik and today. I am in the U.S. now, and yet another one of my friends is suggesting that I write the story down. I write as I remember—a jumble of scenes . . .

We discussed among ourselves the possibility of a war years before it actually started. The Serbian-controlled media said that the city was filled with Ustashas [the state-supported Croatian forces allied with Hitler in World War II and responsible for grave war crimes] and that they presented a threat. We wanted to believe that the city's beauty was going to save it. We could not imagine that in Europe, again, for the third time in the twentieth century, bombs were going to fall on civilians, that there were going to be massacres, that rape was going to be employed on a large scale for territorial gains. Although we saw all the warning signs, we tried to live as if the situation would not deteriorate that far. But it did.

On October 1, 1991, bombs destroyed our transmitters, food supplies, water and electricity installations. We were besieged. Each day was a long struggle for survival. After four days of incessant shelling, some of us decided to take advantage of the Red Cross ferry that promised to bring us to safety.

THE JOURNEY

Day 3, afternoon

My stomach was writhing in my body with the worst seasickness of my life. I put a wet piece of cloth on my face and lay on my side, being as still as possible, trying to calm my frightened body. The bed was damp, one of those very narrow bunk beds in a typical third-class accommodation on Adriatic passenger ships. The mattress was rank with months of refugee service, rank with fear. Under my nose, only a few inches away from my face, were the feet of the other woman in the bed, a nurse, five months pregnant. Since there was not enough room, we lay two to a bed, so her feet were near my face, and her head was near my feet. Every so often she would moan a painful sound from her chest. Every so often she would throw her heavy body across mine and lunge to a small sink in the corner of the cabin to throw up.

On the other lower bunk bed there lay the four-day-old baby. It did not move throughout most of the first leg of the journey. All of us in the cabin had been evacuated from St. Blaise hospital in Dubrovnik. The baby had been sent to safety along with its two-and-a-half-year-old diabetic brother and its mentally retarded mother. From time to time the boy gave instructions to his mother: "Take me up; take me to the bathroom; give me water!" which she would obediently and lovingly fulfill.

This little boy, Ivan, was our hero, taking care of himself, his mother, and his brother. The first time he needed insulin, he approached me and said, "Help me, I need an injection!" He was aware that his mother was not able to do it under the circumstances. Another nurse among the women gave him the insulin. We stared at the little arm, our eyes open, not blinking.

The captain of the ship had left all of his supplies in Dubrovnik. He had expected to stop for food on the way. But once he set sail, he was warned not to stop. In the cabin we dug through our bags for food, taking stock. Ivan's mother had bread, two of us had fruit. We saved as much as possible, because we did not know how long our trip would be.

Day 3, night

Soon after we docked in Zelenika, the ship was met by a brigade of Montenegrin Red Cross ambulances. About five hundred people felt they would not survive the trip and were allowed to disembark. Meanwhile, JNA soldiers came on board, with machine guns on their shoulders, searching every cabin. They were very thorough, precise, yet apathetic. They looked under our beds, poking their guns to see if anyone was hiding there. Under the terms of our passage, no men between eighteen and sixty years of age were allowed to leave the city. All the men who could walk were marched onto the dock, in teeming rain, and left to stand in line. They stood for hours as they were questioned one by one. A few were taken away.

No one knew exactly what was going on, but through word of mouth we managed to get the most important news. We felt trapped in our places and it was very painful not to know what was going on. Those who didn't suffer from seasickness went from cabin to cabin, bringing news. We found out we were sailing from Zelenika the next morning.

Day 4, morning

The ship's engines woke us at dawn. We turned north, having passed the JNA inspection. Even in the rough weather we expected to reach Korcula, our next stop, within several hours. We were promised a safe harbor, water, food and medical supplies, but again we learned we would not be allowed to dock. It was still safe in Korcula, and many people on board had planned to remain there, rest with their relatives or friends, and be close to Dubrovnik. The disappointment was enormous.

The captain's voice came over the loudspeakers again: "I have food for only two hundred meals on board. I have to make a decision how to divide it justly and to avoid panic. We have approximately 3,500 passengers on board. My idea is to put a high price on the food so fewer people will crowd into the restaurant. If anybody on this ship has a better idea, please come forward and let me know." No one had and the food was expensive.

Day 4, daytime

The sea was calmer, so we started talking among ourselves. The main topic was where and how we would live after we got off the ship. At that time we did not know whether the new country we voted for, Croatia, would be recognized as a country or not, what the price would be that we would have to pay for separation.

All the children accepted their hunger; they did not even take a second piece when offered. Preoccupied with thinking about how to make the most of what we had, I handed Ivan a jelly sandwich by mistake. "I don't eat this," he said, looking at me with his big smart eyes. I could not believe there was such perfect sense in the middle of all the humiliation and confusion and despair. For a moment nobody spoke or moved. I know that for everyone there his alertness and simple dignity was a sign of hope that life might somehow continue normally.

THE DESTINATION

Day 4, daytime

We climbed to the top deck, only to see an army cruiser in the distance, following the ship. There was a very old man sitting on a top deck bench, looking at the sea. He had a black coat on and was leaning on a cane. His white hair as well as his beard were flying in the wind, but his face was expressionless. Only his eyes occasionally searched for something in the distance. People would stop to ask him if he was all right, but he would reply in short sentences that he wanted to be left alone. It was cold up there, and somebody brought a blanket to cover his legs.

I knew many of the women on board. Some of them were my colleagues, neighbors, relatives, friends. I kept looking for my friend, a medical doctor, who was working all the time during the trip. She had to disembark her grandmother at Zelenika, because she lost too much liquid with the seasickness and would not survive the rest of the journey. Her parents, however, stayed with her on the ship. At the beginning of the fighting in the Dubrovnik area in autumn that year, the army had burnt their house in the village of Grude, with their dog still inside. The family had already spent months as refugees in Dubrovnik shelters. When I saw my friend on the deck, she was behaving like an automaton, performing perfectly, completely detached from her feelings. There were many who needed her help. There were three deliveries. Two healthy babies and one stillborn were born.

Day 4, night
It was past midnight. My hands were hurting with the heaviness of the luggage I carried down the narrow, steep steps of the ferry, stepping over people and children, to the car department area. Our little group organized itself almost perfectly, trying not to spend any more energy than necessary. Those with children had to be helped because it was impossible to take care of all the things at the same time. Somebody had to carry, others were taking care of the children.

As the people approached the exit, the area in the ship's belly started getting more and more crowded. Finally, there was no more room. We were all standing there, squeezed among our dirty luggage, the wounded, and the crying children. But there was also an immense silence and patience. We had been preparing ourselves for this moment.

THE MEMORIES

Day 1, evening

The feeling in your arms when hugging your mother good-bye. The way you feel her body tensed under the layers of clothes, her soft and fine skin under your fingers, the look in her eyes: many unspoken prayers and the desire to live.

I couldn't decide whether to stay or go. Mother said, "Go."

My mother decided to stay. "I am not leaving," she said, and I knew the decision was final. It was the night two nights before our departure. The air was filled with smoke of the harbor burning. The fire was so big that it made such a light you could see almost as in the daylight, although you were on the other side of the peninsula embracing the harbor.

THE DEPARTURE

Days of exile

To get out of the city was not at all easy. First, you needed to make the decision. Then, you needed a lot of luck. Your name had to be listed on a list made by the Red Cross. Many people stayed because they were so afraid of bombing that they could not risk leaving their shelter to reach the ship. Some others were not ready to wait for the transport for hours and risk being hit by the shelling. The waiting seemed to them much worse than the day-to-day suffering in the shelters.

War taught us a lot. How people change completely, in unexpected and sometimes even unexplainable directions when exposed to it. How the fear makes people irrationally greedy. It is difficult to resist becoming greedy. It is almost like an instinct. To possess, to hold on to something. In shelters, to hold on to somebody. To hold on to your prayer, even if you never prayed before. To hold on to your principles. Then, to give up your principles for the possession. Many know that if they leave, nothing will be there for them to come back to. It will be stolen, taken away, destroyed, burned. To some, their things had meant their life. Old paintings, memories caught in photographs, things they shared together with the dear ones. Their lives would not be complete without these things, and they were prepared to live through all that could come.

THE MORNING BEFORE THE DEPARTURE

Day 3, morning

In the morning we finally had the information that the ship had come in. We had been prepared for the departure since very early in the morning, but we had to wait for hours. On the way to the harbor, we saw a man looking at us while the driver [of the ambulance Vinka and others were traveling in] turned along the curve on the road. The man lifted his hands up to his forehead in a gesture of despair. His eyes were fixed on a woman in the ambulance. "That's my husband," she shouted, and waved. He just kept his eyes pasted on the ambulance. He had a completely lost expression on his face.

I'm holding a four-day-old baby in my arms. "Please, hold the baby," said a nun to me, handing me a small, light-green bundle containing a small, helpless body. "His mother is retarded, and the other kid is a diabetic," said she, and hugged the other child. I had already boarded the overcrowded ambulance in the basement hospital garage after more than thirty-six hours of waiting there for a ship to take us out.

Our vehicle was among the last to reach the ship. The rain was still pouring. I carried the baby in, put him on a piece of luggage, and then started going back for the rest of my stuff. I almost did not make it. The doors were already closing. The captain had a deadline to respect that the JNA had imposed on him, and he was already late. During the embarkation, the JNA promised to hold their fire.

Days 1 and 2

Those hours were filled with anxiety. Would we be able to get to the ship, to get on it, to sail out? We spent time keeping the children calm, talking to each other, worrying.

During the waiting, little things made a difference, like a comforting word, like a sandwich that was handed to me by one of the woman doctors. Her calmness and kindness stayed with me for hours like a shield against all the mess around me. Some of the people gathered there could not communicate—they were in a state of shock. One of them was my friend whose apartment served as a point of strategic defense and where a couple of fighters had died the previous night.

THE ARRIVAL

Day 4, night
The machines came to a stop. The people in the ship were waiting, silent, motionless, for the ship to open its huge belly and let us out. There were so many people that we were afraid that somebody could be hurt. Over the loudspeakers we were warned to wait and to let the first-aid crews carry out the wounded first. It was raining desperately, the same as on the day we embarked in Dubrovnik.

New York, N.Y., U.S.A., June 1994

Although sporadic fighting began earlier, the siege of Dubrovnik began the day after Vinka left Dubrovnik, on October 2, 1991. The JNA bombardment of the UNESCO-protected town—called one of the most beautiful and historic cities in the world—flared on October 23 and again on November 11, continuing throughout the month of December. Unlike the earlier JNA attacks on Vukovar, which were largely ignored by the press, the JNA's shelling of Dubrovnik and the burning and looting of nearby villages drew intense condemnation from the international community.

While a January 1992 agreement calmed the area for a while, Serb shelling continued in May 1992, and it wasn't until October 20, 1992 that the Yugoslav army abandoned its siege of Dubrovnik. Even after that date, however, the city and its surroundings came under periodic attack.

After Vinka wrote this in the United States, she returned to Croatia where she is a psychologist and researcher. She also works on projects to rebuild the destroyed villages near Dubrovnik and to support local refugees.

Merima Nosic, early 30s, Sarajevo

MORE BAGS THAN HANDS

My neighbor drove me as far as Tilave and left me there. Leaving, he whispered to me, "Don't tell anything to anyone, no one needs to know who you are." Those words annoyed me, but I looked around silently. My two children held on to my trousers and I held my ten-month-old baby in my arms. Armed men wearing different uniforms with different symbols stood around me. A helicopter landed on a nearby field and coffins were being slid into it. I shivered, I stood there, hopelessly waiting for some means of transport. My first destination was Pale, where I was to stay the night. I nervously crumpled a piece of paper with the name of the man who could put me up. I had never seen him. All I knew about him was that he was my neighbor's father. A van finally stopped and we managed to get in. There were no seats inside. I put my baby's blanket on the dusty floor so the children could sit down; I sat in the dust.

The journey to Pale lasted for two hours, because we used the long way. We finally reached our destination and got out of the van, white with dust. I turned around, everyone seemed to have somewhere to go and I just stood there confused, not having anywhere to go. A little frightened, I entered a restaurant and politely asked for the telephone. A young man pushed the phone toward me, not asking any questions. I dialed the number and waited. The phone rang but no one answered. I wondered if my host was spending the nice spring day outdoors. Disappointed, I put the phone down and gathered my children and my bags. I had a lot of things because of the children; I could not pick up all the bags with my two hands so I tied them together and began dragging them. We proceeded slowly, but still we moved on.

I walked a hundred meters when a car stopped in front of me. I saw a uniformed man and I stepped back. I recovered, thinking this man does not know who I am. I got in with my children and the man drove me to my destination with no questions asked.

My host was in the yard watching us without interest. In order to get out of an embarrassing situation, I ran up to him and said, "Dusko, you have guests." The man looked at us in disbelief, because he saw a person he had never seen before. I quickly explained who I was and why I was there, quietly so the soldier who was approaching would not notice anything. Our host took our bags and put them under the tree. The grass was green as a carpet, the spring sun was blinding me because I had spent the last forty days in a cellar. I refused the host's offer to go into the house, wanting to breathe the fresh air as long as possible.

He gave us a room and nice clean sheets. I took my clothes off for the first time in a month. I slept dressed at home, never knowing when the shooting would start and when I would need to rush down to the damp cellar with my children. We fell asleep.

At about six o'clock we were awakened by a knocking. Our hostess made coffee and invited me to drink it with her. The good woman insisted on seeing us off despite my protests. When departing, I cried and kissed her as if she was my mother, and as the bus left for Belgrade she waved with tears in her eyes.

The journey was filled with constant police and military checks. No one asked us women anything. A group of people waited for us in Vlasenica, where I was born and through which we passed. I expected to see my only sister in the crowd; she was to give me some money. The driver just rushed by the people, but I saw my sister. My children and I instinctively started shouting to the driver to stop, and a hundred meters later he stopped. My sister ran to the bus and gave me money and a bag of sweets. My sister, together with her husband, was later arrested in Vlasenica and taken to a camp and I still don't know what happened to them. I will always regret that I did not take her with me then.

People around me on the bus talked about the horrors of war; every one had his point of view. I sat confused, watching the places I had once loved so much, now wishing to go away from them as far as possible. I listened to unfamiliar music on the radio. Chetnik songs, I knew, but I had no comment. We had been brought up differently. We had read many books about the Chetniks, Ustashas and other monsters of our people. My God, I wondered where had I come? I wanted to cry but I didn't dare.

A few hours later, the bus stopped on the highway and the driver warned the passengers for Sabac that they had to get out because the bus would not stop in the center of the towns. We got out: the same problem again—how to carry all the bags with just my two hands.

I stood there some time and again I tied the bags together and started dragging them over the dirty and bumpy pavement. People walked by and silently watched, but no one wanted to help. I had very little money so I was not able to pay for a taxi to the bus station. It was a two-kilometer journey and we made it, but I still don't know how I did it.

Tired and sad, we reached the station and I sat down to relax a little. I didn't hurry, all my buses and trains had departed a long time ago. When I pulled myself together a little I went up to buy a ticket for Sremska Mitrovica. The bus was leaving in a few minutes. People pushed in a hurry to get a seat, and I was left with my bags at the end of the line. I had to sit on the dirty and half-torn bags because there were no more seats. People glared at me and I started crying. Nobody asked anything. A younger man approached me and asked me if I was a refugee. I just nodded; I didn't have the courage to look at him. I felt as if I would start to scream. He pushed a crumpled banknote into my hand and told me to buy juice for the children. This made me even sadder and I started wailing loudly. I was not able to control myself.

At the bus station we immediately got on another bus to take us to the village which was our final destination. We passed through a rich village in Sremska Mitrovica, which was near Fruska Gora. The corn had just started to grow, the sunflowers and other plants were bending under the gentle touch of wind. Full-grown wheat seemed like waves on the restless sea. The blood-red sun far away to the west began to set. I watched this sight through the windows of the bus, a sight that could not be seen in Bosnia. There, the still yellow sun sets behind the big mountains. My soul was empty, my eyes dry because I had no more tears.

The house in which I was to live was at the very beginning of the village. My two friends who had left Sarajevo earlier were sitting there while their children were playing in the yard. The driver stopped the bus in front of the house at my request, although it was not the bus stop, and we jumped out immediately. My friends were not surprised to see me because when we had parted in Sarajevo, I had promised them that I would leave the city if the situation deteriorated. We did not need to tell each other anything—our tears said everything.

The arrival of a Muslim woman in a village which was 100 percent Serbian did not pass unnoticed. The men watched me with curiosity and the women with suspicion. My first and only task was to convince them that I came there with good intentions and that I had nothing to do with the war. I began to work diligently. For the first time in my life, I worked with a hoe and I learned quickly as if I had done it all my life. I learned about what it meant to work for a wage although I had only read about it and seen it in films before. I helped older women work in the garden, wash clothes, slaughter pigs and so on. In return they gave me food and clothes.

Life went on, I thought, trying to pretend like it was all right. But it was not all right. People who had come from Bosnia in the 1960s lived in the village. They threatened the owner of the house in which I was staying and other people who were friends with me that they would kill them. My friends did not pay much attention to them. But when I realized that I was creating an embarrassing situation for my host, I tried to find another house in the village where I could live. People in that village are rich and they all had two houses, an old one and a new one. But not one of them wanted to let me live in their property, even in the worst old house without electricity or water. They all found an excuse not to accept me.

When I finally realized what the problem was, I stopped searching for a house, I stopped torturing myself and the villagers.

The more time passed, the clearer it became that I would have to leave. During the summer and fall I could earn enough for my basic needs, because the Red Cross packet was not enough. I was far away from the city and thus far away from what the Red Cross gave others. Winter came and there was not much work. I could not allow others to pay for my needs, so I decided to go. But where? I decided to return to Bosnia. The destination was Fojnica, the house of my friends' parents. But for that journey I needed a passport, because I had to travel through Hungary and Croatia. My Bosnian passport lay in my bag, valid until 1990, and this was 1992. How could I extend the validity when I had no money and did not want to borrow it from others? I decided to sell my husband's wedding ring, the one he had given me when we had parted. The passport pictures cost nine German marks and I could sell the wedding ring for eight marks.

I entered a photo studio and asked the photographer to take our pictures for the cheapest price. I explained our situation and he thought it over for a few seconds and decided to charge me half the usual price. Good people still exist, I thought. That one act of kindness suddenly encouraged me.

I was extensively interrogated by the Ministry of the Interior about my arrival and asked my husband's whereabouts and then I got my passport, which is valid until 1995. I was happy. I had to pack my things again and decide what to take and what to leave. They were all old things, but we needed them. After I had thought about it for a long time, I packed three bags and was ready for the journey.

On April 16—what a coincidence—we left exactly one year after I had left my home before. Our first destination was Novi Sad. From Novi Sad we were to go to Baja, a town in Hungary, and then to Zagreb and Fojnica. We waited at the Yugoslav border for a long time, but we passed without problems. Then came the Hungarian border and the Hungarian customs officer came and inspected the passports. He asked me where I was going. After I explained our situation to him, he demanded a certificate, three hundred German marks, and a letter of guarantee for Croatia. How was I, who barely managed to scrape together the money for the trip, supposed to have three hundred marks? And I didn't have anyone in Croatia who could send me a letter of guarantee. I couldn't understand what was being demanded from me now. The officer left, but he soon came back ordering those of us with the red passport to leave the bus and take our things. The Hungarians didn't like red, but I could not believe that they would not let us continue our journey. At that moment I hated the Hungarians; I watched their blank faces, but not one of them wanted to talk. I gathered my children and my bags again and headed back for Yugoslavia.

All four of us sat helplessly on a bench and cried. Where now? I did not want to go back to the village. People stopped and asked us questions. They all wanted to help. Our stupid Balkan people. In one part of the country they fight and in the other part they want to help. Nobody asked me who or what I was. They all only asked what they could do to help us.

An expensive-looking bus with foreign license plates stopped in front of us and a beautiful lady got out of it. I hadn't seen a such a nicely dressed woman for a long time. She approached us and explained in Serbian that they were from Vojvodina and that they worked in Austria and were going to visit relatives for the Easter holidays. She offered to take us with that bus anywhere we wanted to go. I accepted the offer.

People watched me with curiosity and pity as we got on the bus. They all offered sandwiches, juice, chocolate. The lady next to me cried, saying that she had no children, but that she sympathized with all the victims of this war, especially the children. My children happily unwrapped and ate the chocolate. Their cheeks became stained with chocolate. Let it be, I thought. I didn't even attempt to wipe them. I let them eat. They hadn't seen chocolate for more than a year.

I was thinking where we could go. Sombor, Subotica, or somewhere else? I chose Subotica, not knowing why. When parting, the
woman gave me a few bank notes and some change. I glanced at the
money and smiled. They were German marks. Not much, but
enough to help.

Night fell. I didn't know where to find accommodations. A man
offered to take us to the Red Cross for a fee of five marks. We arrived in front of an old building in the center of Subotica. A man sat
in a big room reading something. I knocked softly and entered, my
boys stained with chocolate coming in after me. When I explained
everything that had happened to me, he phoned someone. I heard
him say: "I have a hopeless case, accept them even for one night."
The man told us that we would spend that night in an orphanage
called the Cradle.

We spent an unforgettable five months there. The lake, Palic, gave
us peace and safety and we felt as if we were at the seaside. We
forgot who we were and why we were there. We walked the city
streets because we were eager for the long-awaited experience and
that excited us. I spent all my free time with abandoned children. I
was especially fond of one-year-old babies. Tragedy was our mutual
bond.

But happiness is always short-lived. The director of the orphanage
decided that refugees could no longer stay there and we had to go
again. We cried. My eldest son had to leave school and his newly
found friends again. The question "Where now?" arose once more.
The answer to that question was easier now that the UN High
Commission for Refugees was taking care of us. The bus came to
pick us up in front of the Cradle and we got in. While riding on
that comfortable bus I remembered my youth and the days when I
was carefree, traveling through our beautiful country. I felt as if I
was traveling to a basketball match or a championship.

We quickly came to a settlement built in a forest. A group of
curious children met us. The driver was in a hurry, not giving us
time to change our mind and go back to Subotica. My friends were

disappointed by the place and protested loudly. I had no choice; I had to stay there. I tried to discover everything that was nice in those surroundings: sports grounds, forests, peace, and the nostalgic sunset. But I was afraid of the people. I was very interested to know what nationality they were. My God, what times these are. Never before had I paid attention to that. The director of the camp explained that these were people of different nationalities and that no one faced discrimination. I soon discovered that the people working in the settlement never did discriminate, but the refugees who lived there did.

As soon as I arrived, my new neighbors greeted me with the words, "A balija arrived, why in our house?" My boys didn't leave our room because they faced constant fights with other children. The kids, like their parents used bad words: balija, Ustasha. I was sorry for my children; they were not strong enough to defend themselves.

The first time the aid workers gave clothes to the children, I was disappointed that my youngest son only got house slippers, because we supposedly did not need other clothes. But my child was happy because the slippers were made to look like a rabbit. Soon after this, a woman came up to me in the middle of lunch and spat at me in front of fifty other people. I heard her say, "You got slippers, you balija, and my grandson didn't. What are you doing here? Your children should go around naked and barefoot." She said some other things but I did not hear her. I felt a buzzing in my head and my whole body began shaking. I thought I would faint; I left lunch and started to run out of the cafeteria. The tears came by themselves. I felt as if most of the people in the cafeteria approved of this behavior and this evil woman.

I felt terrible. I wanted to die, but what would my three small children do? With the help of my new friends I managed to overcome the situation. I used to cry at night often and during the day I would wander aimlessly holding my youngest child's hand. Just when everything had passed and people had begun to forget, a friend whom I saw every day told me that a professor from Sarajevo (another refugee at the camp) threatened her because she was my friend. Sorrow and tears again. Many nights I used to wonder what I did wrong to make people behave toward me in such a way. I knew that my desperation came from the fact that I was not capable of getting used to it. I had lived for so long in a city of love with the greatest possible mixing of ethnicities.

A parcel arrived from the village where I used to stay before New Year. It was sent to me by the people who loved me and who still love me. My happiness was infinite, not because of what was in the parcel, but because I was reminded again that there are people capable of loving regardless of nationality.

Belgrade, Serbia, 1995

The number of Muslim refugees in Serbia is uncountable, because many people with Muslim names do not register themselves officially. Refugee workers in Serbia estimate that from 8 to 15 percent of refugees there are Muslim; the percentage increases dramatically if Serbs married to Muslims are counted.

Merima was a member of the national volleyball team of old Yugoslavia. She wrote this story while sitting on the floor of the Autonomous Women's Center in Belgrade (a group of local refugees and nonrefugees that helps women of all ethnonational groups), waiting to go the airport with her sons. While the youngest son slept, she told the older boys that together they would make a "survival team" in their new country — the United States.

"Brigitte," late 20s, Croatia

THE SUITCASE

After three years of being a refugee, I still can remember how everything happened. And it is as painful now as it was then. I am from Croatia. I used to live there for many happy years. We were

mixed, Croats and Serbs, but in my small town most of the inhabitants were Serbs. When Croatian soldiers tried to enter our town,
the men decided that all women and children should leave the place,
to go to Belgrade. I was confused, but I took my little son and went
to the railway station and we went to Zagreb to catch a train to
Belgrade.

All that spring of 1991, I was dreaming bad dreams, so I wanted
to be awake all the time. I suspected something awful would happen. I was dreaming of blood, weapons, deep gorges, bombs, killing . . . and it seemed real. I wanted to escape from that. Once in my
dream I escaped to a cemetery, a place that I never liked to go even
when awake. Every morning I was happy that it was just a dream,
a nightmare, but I knew I couldn't stand the state of my soul any
longer. I can't escape from my past, it is my life too, it is permanently
interwoven with the present, but I suffer always when I think of
those days.

When we were in a suburb of Zagreb, my son, looking at a [new]
Croatian flag on a house nearby, suddenly said, "Mum, this is not
OUR flag, is it?" My heart stopped beating. There were a lot of people
around us, probably most of them were Croats. I expected to be
arrested, to be thrown out from the train, but fortunately there was
no reaction.

I tried to relax walking around the beautiful park with a lot of
flowers. The railway station in Zagreb is always clean and tidy, and
that day it was the same, but I felt very strange. There were many
people all around, but it was so silent, everybody whispering to each
other and there were a lot of men in uniforms. And there were no
pigeons. Where had they flown away?

Suddenly I realized that a couple of policemen were going from
one person to another at the station asking for their identity cards
and questioning everyone. I could only imagine what would happen
if they saw my documents of a Serb and my intention of going to
Belgrade. My sister noticed them near us but she also couldn't say a

word. We were immobilized, waiting, pretending that we were en-
joying the flowers and our little children. And they came right up
to us. But I heard one of them saying "Diplomacy" as they passed
on. What? Many minutes later, when I could breathe properly again,
I realized what had happened. They had looked at our new nice
suitcase—with the brand name "Diplomatic"—and thought we
were the family of a new diplomat. Until this very day, my son takes
care of that suitcase as if it were a precious relic.

We finally enter the train for Belgrade, our destination as a place
of safety. It was just the outset of our refugee life. We became refugees in our own country.

Belgrade, Serbia, March 1994

*"Brigitte" left Croatia shortly after the Croatian referendum in May 1991,
in which 93 percent of Croats decided that Croatia is a "sovereign and independent country which guarantees cultural autonomy and all civic rights
to Serbs and members of other nationalities in Croatia" and which "may
with other republics join a confederation of sovereign states." Although the
referendum expressly mentioned the rights of Serbs, some ethnic Serbs saw
this language as a threat and a possible demotion from the higher status of
a "nation" equal to Croats to that of a "minority" granted lesser minority
rights. At the same time, Serbs in Croatia were frightened by the reappear-
ance of the checkerboard crest used by the Fascist Ustasha during World
War II—a symbol of Ustasha aggression against Serbs that was forbidden
in Tito's Yugoslavia. Franjo Tudjman's HDZ party (Croatian Democratic
Union) brought a flag sporting the crest back into public view.*

*"Brigitte" chose her pen name to "sound like a movie star," according to
the volunteers who work with her. She refused to use her own name for fear
of reprisal— "from anyone."*

MASS EXIT

The following five narratives were collected from refugees fleeing Krajina (southern Croatia) for Serbia, within hours after their arrival.

Mira Sudzukovic, 60 years old, Lika

We were in bed. It was 4:30 in the morning. The grenades woke us all. The ceiling fell onto us. We didn't have time to dress or even to put on our shoes; we just ran to the cellar. We saw that everything was burning around our house—the tractor, stable . . . Grandfather ran out shouting, "I must save the tractor from the flames." We used the tractor afterwards to come here. I hear that those with tractors will get land.

We didn't dare stay in the village; we had no choice but to run away, because if we stayed it would mean that we would be killed. We took with us only the things we had prepared from before; we didn't have time to pack the things we really needed. We joined the big convoy of everyone from Kordun, Banija, Lika, and Dalmatia. It was the biggest migration of Serbian people: 250,000 were already on the road. We traveled for six days to get to Belgrade. The planes shelled the convoy. People were killed, entire families. Sometimes we had to get off the road, hide in the forest, or go through the field to avoid the shellings.

The army was retreating with us. They had the order to retreat. My son was in the army; he doesn't know why they didn't fight at all. But orders were orders. The soldiers were taking off their uniforms and helping people join the convoy. A man we met didn't know where his family was, but he was helping all the other families. He told me he hoped someone was kind to his family.

Dijana Dobrota, 18 years old, Biovicino Selo (Knin)

This is the second time I have moved. When the war started in former Yugoslavia, I moved from Zadar [Croatia] because I was a Serb. I came to Krajina; I managed to forget my old friends and make some new ones. I forgot even all those horrible things that happened to me in Zadar and I wanted to have a new life in Knin where everybody was kind to me. And now this happened. I don't know if I can start anything again. Here in Belgrade I know nobody, I don't even know if I can start anything again. I don't even know where they will send us. We traveled for six days in the convoy. People were dying, babies were born, and some died. A mother died after giving birth to a baby. I heard that mothers were throwing babies into the arms of the UN soldiers on the road. They thought it would be the only chance for their children to survive.

Ratka, 51 years old, Knin

I live in Germany. I came to Knin for the holidays when this happened. My Croatian friends from Germany told me not to go, that this will happen, but I didn't believe them. I wanted to see my house and my relatives. When the bombing started I was sleeping. I didn't even have time to dress or put on my shoes. I joined the convoy in my nightgown and put on my brother's shoes.

One of my brothers was killed during the Second World War, here in Knin, fighting the Ustashas, and my other brother was killed now again in the same place for the same reason. Isn't this crazy? I never believed that it could happen again after all these years and while we lived all together.

I remember, years ago, I couldn't get my money out of the bank without paying money to the people in charge, because I was a Serb and I needed my money to build a house there. Now I lost the house I had worked all my life in Germany to build. It was a hard life and hard work, you know that. But now it is all over. We have only survival. I have no hope for a new life. They are taking us to Nis, they say. I don't know what will happen there.

Milan Rakic, 10 years old, Knin

I was the youngest soldier in the army; I knew how to use my gun. I am happy about it. I was on the front line; I did it because otherwise I would have been killed. That's why I didn't complain. Now I am safe here. I don't have a gun anymore; even my father gave his gun to the Bosnian army.

Bratko, 30 years old, Knin

Since the beginning of the war I was a soldier in Krajina, but now I wouldn't fight another war even if it was only drinking coffee and having fun. I will throw away my uniform and find myself a peaceful place in the world. I was so excited to fight the war when it all began. But now I know that for every four men who are fighting, six more are sitting in a cafe drinking coffee. While we fought, our leaders drove big cars. I will throw away my uniform as soon as I have some clean clothes.

Raca, Sremska Mitrovica, and Belgrade, Serbia, August 1995

As Yugoslavia began to fall apart at an accelerated pace in 1990, tensions grew in the Krajina — a part of Croatia with a Serb majority. Croatian police officers and territorial defense units (the republic's force) stood opposed to Krajina-Serb paramilitary troops who, Croatian leaders contended, were supported by the largely Serb-controlled JNA. At the end of August 1990, after a two-week referendum, the Krajina Serbs declared their autonomy from Croatia. On February 28, 1991, the government of the self-proclaimed "Serbian Republic of Krajina" adopted a resolution to form an independent state that in the future would join Serbia. The worst clash in ex-Yugoslavia since World War II took place two months later in Krajina, a dispute purportedly over the flying of the Serbian flag (although disputants on both sides claim the incident was "staged"). Thirteen police officers and four civilians died. The next day, JNA tanks occupied Borovo Selo and nearby towns and Croatian President Franjo Tudjman announced that "open war" had begun. After this point, Croat-Serb fighting over Krajina continued for over four years, with Krajina Serbs retaining control.

In August 1995, in an operation termed "Storm," Croatian troops retook Krajina, sending over 250,000 refugees fleeing across Bosnia-Herzegovina. Most ended up in Serbia. The line of humanity was not only the largest single refugee flow of the war, it was the most unusual as well, as men joined the refugees in record numbers. "We are a state on the road," one Krajina fighter remarked, surveying the exodus. Only the elderly and infirm remained behind. In October 1995, journalists and human rights workers reported that many of the remaining elderly Krajina Serbs had been murdered by Croats. At the same time, independent journalists within Serbia reported that some of the newly arrived Krajina Serbs had taken the homes of ethnic Croats, forcing some Croat families in Serbia to flee.

The Krajina refugees who spoke to us were still in a state of shock. They could hardly talk without crying. Because they had had no time to prepare themselves for leaving home, they were all dressed in inappropriate clothing: slippers, nightgowns, working clothes, woolen sweaters on a hot summer day.

Subhija Salic, 60 years old, Sarajevo

PEOPLE ARE ALWAYS THE SAME

My neighbor, a Serbian woman, took me out of town . . . the people are always the same. We were all the same in the building. We would run together to the cellar: we didn't insult each other. When Arkan and Seselj came to Grbavica [Sarajevo], the Serbs also were frightened, and my neighbor, this Serbian woman, told me that I must get out and flee. My husband left town the next day; I left everything in the house, I just took an empty handbag so they wouldn't notice that I was running away. Every one of those soldiers, the Chetniks, were drunk. We pretended that we saw nobody and that we heard nobody. I pretended to go out to buy milk. I just crossed the bridge and I stayed in my son's one-room apartment.

Later on my friends found a place for me to stay. My husband came out too. I came to America after the death of my husband. I feel bad in America; I miss Bosnia, we don't have money, we don't speak the language, we are old. They help us but we are surviving, not living. We had a wonderful life; we will never be like we used to be. I would go back immediately if only the war stopped. Only that one bridge divides the Serbian part from the Bosnian part of the city of Sarajevo, and people are, as I said, always the same.

Once I was expecting a visitor from Grbavica [a Serb-held part of Sarajevo] on the Bosnian side of the bridge. A Serbian woman whom I didn't know tried to cross the bridge from the [Serbian] side. She trembled with fear, she had heard terrible stories of what was going on our side and she suddenly stopped in the middle of the bridge. She dropped everything from her hands and trembled frightfully. I went out to her. She had to cross the bridge in order to see her daughters. She had heard they had been killed. She didn't dare go forward. I told her we would call her daughters to reassure her. I did it and only then did she cross the bridge.

People are always the same. We were 150 lodgers in my building, of all nationalities and we all baked bread on the stove of a Muslim woman and we divided it every day.

St. Louis, Mo., U.S.A., 1995

When Subhija speaks of the Serb and Muslim parts of Sarajevo, she refers to sectors created after the war began. Before the war, residents of all ethno-national groups lived side by side throughout most of Sarajevo. Residents of big cities like Sarajevo and Mostar (another multicultural city in Bosnia that fell under siege during the war) were among those most likely to iden-tify themselves as "Yugoslav" — instead of "Croat," "Serb," "Muslim," or something else. In the 1981 Yugoslav census, 83 percent of the people in Bosnia who identified themselves as "Yugoslav" lived in cities. Seselj is the extreme right-wing nationalist founder of the Serbian Radical party — a neofascist advocate of "ethnic cleansing."

Subhija left Sarajevo on July 7, 1994 for the United States. Like the other Bosnians in St. Louis, she can be seen regularly at the Bosnian Club.

DREAMS OF HOME

"Always, in the corner of your mind, you have Bosnia, and if you can forget it for a period of time, that is a very short time."

"I never want to forget my town. The worst thing for me is that my children will probably forget."

"Were our customs really beautiful, or am I just imagining things?"

ne can never stop dreaming, the urge for fantasy can never be killed even when darkness covers every corner of one's reality. Dreams of horror. Dreams of happiness. What was and what could have been. Life's law of balance. The soul's need to surrender into something both fantastical and free. A sometimes forgotten law: bad things as well as good must somehow come to an end. Refugees push aside their nightmare of being killed, raped, tortured at home for fantasies of the place that once and forever in their memory will be their home. The emotion that colors their dreams is homeland, motherland—whatever it was, whatever the mother.

Refugees' dreams carry a heavy burden: they provide the only true home, the intact memory of what used to be and what is lost forever. The smallest things that make us alive can become the most powerful dreams. When a woman dreams of watering her violets, she remembers the light on her terrace, the smell of air in her home, that love of life that makes flowers as important as humans. Or, in their innocence, more important.

When your dignity is threatened every day, remembering becomes a heroic, transformative act. When lovers write letters that all authorities will read, crudely violating the intimacy, then the syrupy language of love, obsessive and repetitive, becomes a political act. "You can take our letters, our homes, our land, and even our family," the letter writer declares, "but you cannot destroy our dreams, our

love." When refugees pass around postcards and photographs of
their homes and even build models of their towns, they are shouting,
"I remember. And this memory you can never take from me."

Saja Atic, 50 years old, Olovo

I REMEMBER

I remember my neighbor, Hodzic Taiba. We used
to sit for hours in front of the house and talk talk
talk . . . Who would ever know all that we talked
about. And we laughed. Still now I wear the blue
scarf that Taiba gave to me. Before she escaped with
her daughter to Munich, she gave this blue scarf as
a gift to me. She had blue eyes like the scarf.
"When I return we shall go together to have
hamburgers at Asim Place. And we shall keep all the stories
so that we have something to laugh about. Take care."

Taiba, my best neighbor. Same as my sister. Even
more. That is why I am silent now and I keep all
the beautiful stories for us. So when she comes back
we shall have something to laugh about.

Belgrade, Serbia, 1994

*Saja Atic left Olovo for Belgrade in 1993. While in Belgrade, she met local
women working against the war and for the rights of refugees. She wrote
this poem in a writing workshop of Women in Black, the women's peace
group from Belgrade that stood in protest every week in the middle of the
city, to the jeers of onlookers and under constant harassment by police.
Women in Black also worked on humanitarian aid projects for refugees,
regardless of their ethnonational group, including refugee handicraft projects
and emergency aid. This poem was the inspiration for Rada Zarkovic, a
refugee from Mostar, to make a collection of refugee stories entitled "I Remember," published by Women in Black in Belgrade.*

Jasenka and Suki, middle aged, Sarajevo

BIRTHDAY GREETINGS

My dear friend:

With this small bunch of violets I send you my best and sincere wishes for your birthday.

Please, don't be sad today. You really should have been born, for yourself, for me and for all the others you are giving love to, that human love: unselfish love.

I needed you and I will always need you as a friend and good person. I feel great when I think that you exist and that you think of me, especially now in this crazy life.

When you say cheerio tonight (with our Babic wine), let the first best wish be mine for your health and happiness and for our being together again. I would love to offer a toast here too but I have nothing except plain water, and I am afraid that even water isn't healthy anymore.

Be still happier and healthier, and possibly both.

My dear, for this time this is all. We are relatively OK. I am still spending dull time at home. I cure myself with books and water, in order not to go crazy. Suki works every day. Nothing nice happens, so there is nothing I can write to you about.

Best regards to everybody, I wish I was with you.

Once again all the best in your future life.

Yours,
Jasenka and Suki

Sarajevo, Bosnia-Herzegovina, July 1995

The authors of this letter sent it to their dear friend, who had been a refugee in Zagreb for over two years. A friend of the "birthday girl" from the women's center at which she works translated this letter and urged the editors to include it in this collection. "We have so many of these letters," she sighed; "people forget about the decision to leave — about the friends left behind." The "birthday girl" said that Jasenka and Suki have always managed to send her notes encouraging her in her new life.

Dusanka Maric, late 60s, Bosnia-Herzegovina

MEMORY

It was late in the afternoon. I was packing the most needed things. She followed me. She went after me from one room to another. She shuffled around my legs. My cat Mira, as if she knew I was leaving. Yes, she knew it very well.

When I took my bags she went after me. I told her: "Stay there, Mira, watch our house. Luka and I are leaving. Even though we don't know where we are going."

Mira stopped. She stopped and followed me with her eyes. I walked and looked back nobody knows how many times, and she was still there, on the same spot, watching us. I started to cry. I cried while walking. We were far away. I couldn't see her anymore, but I could see her and her eyes as if she were before me.

Belgrade, Serbia, 1995

This is the first and only story Dusanka Maric has ever written.

Nada Ristic, 44 years old, Jesanj Mikula

ZADA

The telephone rang. Oh that telephone! Who knows how many times it rings daily. I am simply scared of it these days. No, it was not crisis headquarters that time. It was Zada, my neighbor who invited me for a cup of coffee.

My neighbor Zada used to drop in very often. She was a little bit younger, serene, she was full of gentleness and humor. She used to find something humorous in ordinary things. It was a pleasure to drink a cup of coffee chatting with her. She was my recreation, someone who broke my worries, as we would say. But these days, these hard days everything has changed, even Zada. We had a cup of coffee and talked about the war. Zada and me, we asked ourselves could it be possible? We were sad and teary-eyed. We had our coffee and we cried a lot, me and Zada. I had never seen Zada sad. I had never seen her crying because she was always serene and full of joy. But that day her tears could not stop. We cried and drank the coffee, which was cold, and her two sons played around us. I had no idea that it was our last coffee. It was the last day in my neighborhood and the last coffee with Zada. I believe that I will never have such a friend again.

Belgrade, Serbia, 1995

Nada was a dedicated teacher in Bosnia-Herzegovina. According to the volunteer counselor who worked with her, Nada faced a "major psychological crisis when she first got to the refugee camp, but she managed to break out of it." Even today, she still shows people pictures of her class, and she constantly speaks fondly about the past. As of this writing, she still lives in a refugee camp near Belgrade.

Mirsada, 38 years old, Brcko

FOR MY FRIENDS

April 26: I crossed the bridge. Sometime earlier I had taken the children across the bridge and left them in Bunja. I went back to get some things, but then I couldn't cross the bridge anymore. My daughter lost consciousness; she thought I had left her for good. They had to give her medicines. So I raised my hands one day and crossed the bridge. I risked my life, but I had to for the sake of my children.

We came to Vienna, where I had my third child. We managed to bring a lot of our relatives here. But it is hard to tell you about our life. I would go back immediately if I could give something to eat to this baby of mine. I worked in a shoe factory for years and I loved my job. I would work now for free if only the factory still existed, but it was torn down to the ground.

I had more Serbian than Muslim girlfriends. They would always bring me eggs and cakes, but I cannot reach some of them anymore and I miss them. I would like to help them because I know what they are going through. And if I were there we would still be friends; we were not afraid of anything. We believed so much in each other, but this war destroyed everything. I don't know who made this war, but I know that tomorrow these people will again live together.

Vienna, Austria, May 1995

Brcko, a city in Bosnia-Herzegovina on the border with Croatia, was the site of intense fighting throughout the war. In May–June 1992, Serb paramilitary troops murdered between 2,000 and 3,000 Muslims in the Brcko environs. Mirsada brought her children to safety shortly after that, but she remained behind until April 1993. She traveled through Croatia to Austria, where local refugee workers helped her find housing.

This story was transcribed by Slavica Stojanovic, who visited her on a hot spring day. Mirsada had brought her two-month-old baby to a neighbor's home, to allow her to speak in peace. "She was talking freely," Slavica remembers, "telling me how much she loved her friends and how she tried to send them letters. When we were leaving she told us we should be her guests next time in Vienna."

Woman, 41 years old, Mostar

IN MILAN

Every morning, I wake up remembering the same dream. I am five, I have short hair as my mummy used to cut it for me, with an uneven fringe because I could not stay still. I am sitting on a small baby-bed covered with a green, coarse handmade rug. I am calm, happy, and alone. Everybody has gone somewhere. I try to stand up and I realize that my bed is moving; it rises slowly as if lifted by an invisible hand from the sky. Slowly but steadily it moves toward the window, then it escapes through the window and up into the clouds.

Finally I fly, riding my baby-bed. I look out and see my town: the river, the park, my friends in the courtyard, Father driving the car, Mother waiting with her arms full from shopping. I pass them all very quickly because we move quickly, toward somewhere else, sucked in by a strong but not dangerous tornado. And my town is out of sight and I feel big and grown up, and I wake up.

Of my town, I remember mostly simple things: the way some people walked and talked loudly on the streets, eating or embracing or fighting. People here in Milan are quiet; they dress as the calendar regulates and they rarely express their emotions or pleasures publicly.

Of my town, I remember the kitsch blue sky and clouds of funny shapes. It would rain in the sunshine and snow on the first of May. Local people called it crazy weather; foreigners took special precautions to survive nature's mood. In Milan you can't see the sky. The air is not transparent, the clouds are one big cloud called a cap (winter cap and summer cap), and the rain falls from nowhere. But it is a stable and well-balanced climate. Once you get used to it, it provides a certain grim security.

Of my town, I remember some of my relatives who are not alive anymore. My aunt would prepare wonderful Turkish coffee every afternoon. The things we discussed while drinking that coffee were never those one says on other occasions: it wasn't gossip, it wasn't intimacy, it wasn't work. It was coffee talk. Without that coffee you could not make that talk, not even reproduce it. In Milan I wouldn't dream of making Turkish coffee. Everybody would laugh at me and make me feel stupid. Here coffee is called espresso and people drink it standing up, in a big hurry at a bar. They just drink it in silence, turn around and go for their work. I would never ask anything, not even what time it is to somebody who is drinking espresso in Milan. That would be rude.

But there are many things I don't remember anymore about my town. They fade away, they slip into some other memory file, they melt into different emotions, smells, colors, sounds of a different life, of a different world and of a different me. In Milan I am alone, strong and new. I an independent, self-sufficient and aware of many things I had never known before. I am not happy because I don't believe in happiness. My memory of happiness has faded away. In Milan people are happy without knowing it.

Milan, Italy, 1995

A large number of people from all parts of ex-Yugoslavia have sought refuge in Italy. Many are not counted. Having arrived as tourists, they simply stayed on, taking jobs where they could, staying with friends to make ends meet. According to the refugees themselves, Italy has since made entry requirements much more difficult in order to discourage new arrivals. In northern Italy, the editors met refugees mainly in bars — bars known as the Serbian bar, Bosnian bar, or, simply, Refugee bar. Most refugees did not want to give their stories. A woman with two little girls said, "I have even lost faith in humanitarian aid. I have a feeling that even people who are helping us are doing it for themselves and not for us. That is why I want to forget my story and never tell it to anyone again. I don't even feel like a refugee anymore. I just feel poor." Only one woman would write her story.

This woman comes from the sector of multicultural Mostar now known as the Muslim sector. In October 1992, Bosnian Croat forces captured Mostar, declaring it the capital of the Croatian Union of Herzeg-Bosna. According to UN refugee personnel and international human rights advocates, the conditions of the Croat-run detention camp for Muslims near Mostar grossly violated standards of international humanitarian law. Although the rebuilding of Mostar had already begun at the time of this writing, the author had little hope of ever returning.

Adisa, Nasir, Hajra, Muriz, Mirsada, Remzija, Melisa, Senid, Aziz, Uzeir, Mevlida, Sahza, ages 13 to early 50s, Sarajevo, Jajce, and Donji Vakuf

I BELIEVED: GROUP POEM #1

I used to believe that the world was full of many colors
now I know it's just black.

I used to believe that all people are kind
now I know only some of them are.

I used to believe that my friends would be with me all of my life
now I know that none of them would give any part of their body
    for me.

I used to believe that I could trust people
now I know that I should be careful.

I used to believe that people made friends to help people
but now I know people make friends out of self-interest.

I used to believe that I would have a good life with my neighbors
but now I know it is easy for them to kill in war.

I used to believe that no one could force me away from my homeland
but now I know this isn't a dream.

I couldn't believe that my generation could be worse than the older
    generation
but now I know they are.

I used to believe in everything
but now I believe in nothing.

I used to believe in happiness
but now I cannot even believe my eyes.

I used to believe that I would live by my wishes
but now I know I will live by other people's wishes.

What I couldn't believe, I now believe.

IF I COULD BE STANDING: GROUP POEM #2

If I could be standing anywhere,
I would be
    on my balcony, calling my children in for lunch;
    on the top of the old castle in Jajce, looking from above at
        my town;
    on a plane going home;

in a small house with a big yard where my children could play
   without fear;
in my house with my husband and daughters, talking and
   drinking coffee;
in front of my television with friends dropping by to say hello;
in Bosnian forests with Bosnian rivers floating by;
at the grave of my father;
anyplace where my children would be safe;
swimming in a lake in my town;
walking and chatting with friends;
playing ball with the boys in my yard;
standing in all places of my town at the same time.

I would not be standing.
I would be a bird
   flying above my country,
   never before did I realize how much I love her
   and that she is so beautiful.

I would be turning back the clock,
   returning and reliving my past life
   —I know it will never happen again.

Islamabad, Pakistan, August 1995

*These two poems were written by Bosnian refugees in Pakistan as part of a
writing workshop conducted by Julie Mertus and Eve Ensler. The group of
Bosnians and their two American guests sat around in a circle on the floor,
sipping coffee and smoking cigarettes. Eve suggested that the group make a
poem together: Fill in the blank: "I used to believe ————, but now I know
————." After an embarrassed silence, Nasir sighed, "It has been such a
long time since someone asked us to think." But then, after an even longer
silence, he began. Julie transcribed and "mediated" the poem, sharing it with
the group for their comments and corrections.*

   *By the time the group made its second group poem, everyone wanted to
chime in. The assignment was to complete the thought, "If I could be standing
anywhere, ————." Again, Eve created the exercise and Julie transcribed.*

The person who said he wanted to be "on a plane going home" was a four-year-old boy. The only plane he had ever been on had taken him to Pakistan.

All of the participants in the group poems had been waiting over a year for a visa to the United States. Their trip had been held up by bureaucracy: there wasn't enough money in last year's budget for an asylum adjudicator to visit their camp, the official at the U.S. embassy in Islamabad explained. Seven months after they made these poems, they all made it to the United States. Apart from some of the teenagers in the families, all of them now want to return home.

Ljiljana Trkulja, 23 years old, Tuzla

TUZLA

Trice[1]: reality ceases in my eyes,
under the last twinkling of a wandering star
longing is in the place of reality,
dashes on the wings of dream.

Uncoil by my sight familiar streets, passersby, childhood,
again I am where I belong, where my soul
has been left, my heart bleeds;
but, human's hatred has done its job.

Zero, forgotten, left; I smell the burning,
I see the ruins, the rain I think, but it is an explosion,
a child searches for his brother.

Lingering, I close my eyes, and ask myself is it a dream
or reality. I understand, nobody could start life
anew nor from a dream could live, past time . . .
I turn my eyes with tears for a city,
I leave the past for the dream is mixing with
reality.

1. "Trice" is a Serbian word meaning something useless, meaningless, worthless, senseless.

Again, the pain and longing is still in me; no return,
there is no future.
Emptiness alone.
Hence, I ask you only: DON'T ASK ME
HOW I AM AND HOW I LIVE.

Mala Krsna Camp, Serbia, 1994

Tuzla was under siege for up to seven months at a time in 1992, choking residents off from food and supplies. The city became a Muslim-controlled stronghold, serving as a focal point for humanitarian aid operations and a reception area for refugees in flight. At the same time, the shelling of Tuzla and its environs continued sporadically. In the spring of 1995, a large group of young people were killed after the shelling of a Tuzla cafe.

Most Serbs who left Tuzla did so early in the war. Ljiljana had been in a refugee camp near Belgrade for over a year when she wrote this poem. A local peace worker who had befriended Ljiljana said that she "talks and behaves as if she never left Tuzla. She speaks in the present tense and dreams of going back home."

Ljubica Trkulja, 53 years old, Tuzla

VIOLETS

I remember my violets that remained blooming on the window of my kitchen. And all the flowers too. My violets flourished in various colors: blue, pink, white. I watched them there one next to the other as in a conversation, not knowing that I would go forever, and that my hand would not water them and nourish them any more. Oh, God, where is the end of this hell, when will I have violets and other flowers in my flat again? I always think how my violets dehydrated and died, dropping their gorgeous flowers.

Belgrade, Serbia, 1995

Ljubica Trkulja writes constantly, signing each piece with her full name and address — that is, her address from Tuzla, complete with the floor and door number. She has lived in a refugee camp near Belgrade for over two years. She vows to return.

Iris Kusalsic, Bosnia-Herzegovina

SJECANJA (MEMORIES)

There! I have landed like a seed
carried by the wind. Only the roots—
didn't spread yet. My soul is dying out.
From a familiar scent, far away I am, separated.
My heart hurts, still bleeding, and still
dreaming of returning.

Sometimes, it seems, I begin
to forget. The images fade away
disappearing from the mind, but
some gesture, a well-known sign,
arouses again the bitterness of parting.
And I am alone. The winds
have blown me away. God! I know not
where I shall end up.

To one side, the remembrances urge me
onward but the current will not let me.
I lose the sight of you . . .

Philadelphia, Penn., U.S.A., 1994

This was one of the first contributions to The Suitcase. *Somehow, it made its way to the editors through a friend of a friend of a friend. The translation was done by Emir Pasalic.*

Zorica Milutinovic, 16 years old, Dubrovnik

TO DUBROVNIK

Deserted my heart is now without you, far away you are now,
as there is nobody, as there is nothing.

Up in the bright heaven—there is your place,
your white towers would be a pearl of this planet.

Brightness of yours will be the strongest,
pearls from the sea will enjewel the gates of Heaven.

Ruler of yours is paradise, the word of God is working.

Oh how beautiful you are, how much I miss you,
and maybe everything is just a dream.

Very high is my desire,
I would like to come back to you.

Nobody like you, there my soul found
eternal peace.

In time when my face disappears . . .

Keen I am of you, and when everything wipes off
I will come again because I cannot be without you.

Pristina, Kosovo, November 1994

Most of the refugees in Kosovo (the troubled southern region of ex-Yugoslavia which is 90 percent ethnic Albanian and 10 percent ethnic Serbian) have the look of zombies — the downward cast of beaten men and women, lost and without hope. Given the ever-present tension between ethnic Serbs and ethnic Albanians in Kosovo, it is a strange destination for a Serb fleeing conflict. But many of the refugees in Kosovo had been persuaded to come by the promise of employment and housing. Once they arrived, however, neither housing nor the promised job materialized, and they ended up in deserted workers' camps and closed (mainly formerly Albanian) school houses.

Zorica is the one bright light in her camp. Her room — her own cubicle — is plastered with posters of rock stars and puppy dogs and festooned with every beautiful thing that has come into her life — a soft bar of soap, a new brush, a hair tie — all neatly displayed as on an altar. In the camp, Zorica is known as "the writer." This poem was written by hand in a wide-lined notebook, decorated with dreamy photographs cut from glossy magazines.

Hodzic Raska, 58 years old, Sarajevo

I WATCHED CHILDREN PLAY THROUGH MY WINDOW

I lived on the border line between the two sides. They kept bombing us. It wouldn't stop. A sniper hit the sink in my kitchen. I kept standing by the window seeing all kinds of things; I didn't dare go out. One day as I was watching, some children gathered in front of a wire fence behind which was UNPROFOR, and they were giving them chocolate. A bomb fell in their midst, killing the children, mutilating them. Nobody ever said a word about that.

I couldn't watch anymore through my window. I couldn't hide anymore. There was no food, there was no water.

They built the Blue road, the UN troops, and our government gave permits to people older than fifty-five to leave the town. By then, I already had two daughters in the U.S.A. I went first to Zenica. From Zenica I went to the Croatian border, to Kamensko. There I spent five days; they didn't let me into Croatia because I didn't have a visa. How could I find a visa? Who would give me a visa from Croatia? I sold my ring for one hundred German marks and I paid some *mafioso* to drive me to Imotsko. I thought I would die. I was so sick. I traveled clandestinely as far as Split. They kept asking for papers all the time—I had to avoid it. I don't know how I did it. I was given food by the truck drivers on the road who felt sorry for me. Somehow I got to Split, then to Zagreb, and there my American visa was waiting for me.

My husband stayed in Sarajevo. He cannot come out. I'm glad that I am here with my children but I miss my country and my town. I will go back as soon as things settle down.

St. Louis, Mo., U.S.A., April 1995

Hodzic spoke in a sad, low voice while she sipped her coffee at the Bosnian Club. She couldn't wait to get back home.

Ferida Durakovic, Sarajevo

EVERY MOTHER IS A GIFTED CHILD

When we rushed out of our homes into the city, perhaps forever, I took some of my favorite books, a checkered vanity case, and undergarments. She carried two bags filled with food. I ask, Mother, what did you bring? That which everyone needs, she says. Later between the shelling and sniper shots she went to our garden and brought us lettuce, onions, and carrots. Are you afraid? I ask. No, my love, she says. I think only of my children and God shows me the way. THERE.

When they stationed my brother by our home, she dressed herself nicely and went to see him. Where are you going, Mother, for God's sake? I ask, distressed. I am going to help him, to make it easier for him, she says. My brother barely broke out alive from the enemy enclave. Don't, my mother says, for God's sake, help me any more. Now she sits all day on the balcony, watching and listening. Is he alive? Maybe he is lying on the ground? Does he have anything to eat? . . . Do you recall the ridiculous mother of Nikoletina Bursac—eh, exactly like that. Just a little different. THERE.

When I found accommodations for the two of us, after our stay on the fifteenth floor, on the ninth floor with friends, she says to me, as if she is guilty of some crime: You know, love, I have to organize myself in this kitchen. But I memorized where things are, so when we return home (!) if God allows us, I will put everything back in its place. THERE.

The other day as I am coming back from my rounds through the city, it's as though I am passing through a never-ending grave, and I count: first, third, fifth, seventh, ninth floor, and I come across a barrier made of rope. She opens the door. I ask, What is it, Mother? She says, I tied it so that you know when you have reached our door.

Early in the afternoon she lights the oil lamp in the stairwell, so that people see what they are bumping into. She keeps the door to the apartment open, so the neighbors do not saunter aimlessly through the ebony sky. She leaves matches by my bed, on shelves, on tables. She wakes up in the middle of the night to relight the oil lamp in the hall: she knows I fear the dark; this way the light finds its way near my side. She doesn't sleep at all; instead her crazy motherly instinct keeps her up all night, her ear stretches across the building to check if we are breathing, whether we are appeased, having bad dreams, in pain. THERE.

All day long, nine floors up and nine floors down, she brings water. Before the war she couldn't even climb nine steps. Now it's as though nothing hurts. Only that she has dropped two sizes. Now, she says, I cannot be in pain, there is war. Later I will be as sick as I please. A couple of days ago an acquaintance asked me: How do you manage to stay so clean and white without any water or electricity? She's to blame, I say. She fetches water, washes all my white shirts, sterilizes my pants and running shoes, and dries them. Then she prays to God for just a little electricity, quickly she irons and hangs the clothes in the armoire. You mustn't, she says, look like a refugee, out of spite to those who chased us out of our homes. THERE.

When shots are heard above the skyscrapers, we argue. I say, I won't go to the stairwell, nor to the basement; I feel better when I read during the shelling. Fine, she says, I am staying with you. And she sits by my side, but I know she is scared to death. She sits until I become so completely infuriated that I comply and go to the stairwell or basement. I have never seen anyone quite so stubborn in my life. She will make sure that I am safe or she will not be. THERE.

Around the beginning of the war I find her under the house, sitting on a bag of sand and crying. What is it? I ask. "Ma'nako!" [just so], she says. What do you mean, "'nako?" I ask. Well, she says, I am ashamed that I gave birth to you. But why, Mother, we are not so terrible, I kid her. It's not that, she says seriously, I am ashamed that I brought you into such a world. If I knew, she says, that I would have to die for this war to end, I would lay down there and die. Just so that my children and grandchildren would survive. THERE.

God and I have a divineless, calculated relationship. Not her. Of all material interests she prays only to once again have us all gathered around, alive and well, in her home with its entrance into the city, and to bring out her special strudel that we made every Saturday, leaving the dishes for her to wash and straighten up the mess that only her grandchildren can get away with. THERE.

She nags me everyday, that I don't know how to make the best of a situation, that I am naive . . . I don't know how to answer her, so I say: You know, Mother, I am a poet, that's why. You're Mummy's little lamb, she says. She smothers me with kisses. THERE.

She is always, persistently dreaming the same dream: How she returns home, the house in perfect condition, her flowers blooming, the cat sleeping on the old chair on the verandah, she is walking out of the house refreshed, showered, it's Saturday and we are on our way home for lunch, and in the evening we are having barbecue, and she cannot seem to keep up, and she starts to feel smothered, oh God, anxiety sets in and she wakes up—to a crazy war, sweaty and afraid, in somebody else's home, in somebody else's bed, and just over there, across the sky, the grumbling shelling tearing her heart apart piece by piece. God, if you would live long, my dear elder. You endure, and so will I. For only with you will this war, like some everlasting and grave sickness, end; you will embrace it with your secret balm made of wisdom and healing herbs. And from your old folk tales where—one must relate—the winner is always the one who does not harm nor wish harm upon others.

Ferida Durakovic is a writer from Sarajevo. She contributed this to Izi: Refugees for Refugees, *a refugee-run magazine published in Ljubljana, Slovenia.*

Slovenia was the first republic of the old Yugoslavia to declare its independence and, as a result, also the first site of a clash between a "territorial defense unit" and the Yugoslav army (JNA). The entire battle took roughly a week, during July 1991. On July 2, the Yugoslav air force bombed Ljubljana, Slovenia's capital—but by July 8, the war was over; later that month, the JNA pulled out for good.

Hajrija, 42 years old, Donji Vakuf

MODEL TOWN

The first thing I think about is entering the door of my house. I imagine I am walking on the streets with my friends. I imagine that I am putting on make-up and some new clothes to go to a party with my friends.

When you enter our town, on the left side you'll see a tower with a clock. I looked at this tower every day of my life, so did all my relatives as long as anyone can remember. In the very center of the town, you'll also see a beautiful place for walking and a big square. There is a mosque and a church and a hotel. There are a lot of flowers around. I never want to forget my town. The worst thing for me is that my children will probably forget.

My husband made a model of our town to keep the memory alive. A few men have made models in this camp. I don't know what happens to them when their families move away. One family just left for Australia—I think they left their town in the middle of their room.

It takes a long time to build a town because it isn't easy to find the right materials here [in Pakistan]. We had to have red roofs on the houses and lots of green for the trees. The green was particularly hard to find. My husband was very determined. He looked and looked and finally we found some branches that we could cut to look like small trees. We must tend the model all the time because the green turns yellow. My husband made the clock tower separately, so it could sit alone above the town, just like at home.

There is a retarded girl from our town who is in this refugee camp. When she saw the clock tower, she began to cry. She hugged the tower so tight, we couldn't make her let it go. Of course we let her bring it to her room. She won't let it out of her sight; she sleeps with it at night. Sometimes when she comes to visit, she brings the clock tower, and then the town and tower are together again.

Islamabad, Pakistan, August 1994

The model town — Donji Vakuf — was overrun by Serbs at the beginning of the war. Hajrija's family had lived in Donji Vakuf as long as anyone could remember. Same with her husband's family. "No one every thought of living anywhere else," she said. The inscription on the model town reads: "These are our houses, on the land inhabited by our forefathers, we are going back there no matter when and in such a way that we'll be so powerful that no one will be able to force us to leave our land again."

Hajrija now lives with her family in Utica, N.Y. The model town remains in Pakistan.

Mr. K., 57 years old, Turic

LAND

Now I live here with my family in Germany but of course my wish is to go home sometime. You can only hope this will be possible. But it doesn't look good. Even if we never have that which we had, even if we had to live in a self-built shack, the main thing is that you are on your own piece of land. As an old saying goes, land which is not your own brings another man's grief and pain.

I remember several things I saw in the destroyed villages. Once when I wanted to go home from the front, I saw a cow that was hit by a grenade. It was lying still on the ground and a little calf was next to it, trying and trying to get some milk from its mother. But of course it couldn't achieve anything. It was a horrible picture.

Then I arrived at my house and saw everything had been destroyed. All I thought was, oh my God, what has happened?

I am an old man and I've lost everything, my home, my place, my land. What hope remains for me now?

Hermannsburg, Germany, 1994

This story arrived for The Suitcase *as if by magic, coming by mail as the final manuscript was being completed. Rev. Klaus Burckhardt sent a bundle of stories from Germany. No one is quite sure how the reverend found* The Suitcase.

Woman, 54 years old, Knin

DREAM ON THE PAVEMENT

During the trip my younger son was lost somewhere in the convoy. My other son died before the war, so he is all we have. So here we are, my husband and me, and we are not moving from our spot on the pavement because this is the place where all refugees come, and my son must come here too. If I lose him now I am afraid that we will never meet again. They are trying to get me into a bus to take me somewhere else, but I will not move. I will wait one hundred more days until I find my son.

I am very tired. I can't sleep at night so I doze off during the day. Listen to the dream I had only a few hours ago. I am going with my girlfriend back to Knin. Something is dragging me toward my house. My girlfriend says she doesn't want to go with me any further because she is afraid of the Croatian soldiers. So she stays behind near a river. I go very near my house; the lights are on inside. I don't have my key. I decide to break in because I want to find the photograph of my dead son. I had forgotten to take it with me in all the rush. And then I see that all the animals have been slaughtered: my cat, my dog, my hens, my cow. At that moment a man gets ahold of me from the back and puts his knife against my throat. I say to him, "Don't cut my throat. I have nothing to do with any army, ours or yours. No man in my family fought in the war." Then another man with a long beard, hearing my words, tells the first man, "OK, we won't cut her throat. We will grant her death by poison." And he pulls out a long needle and sticks it into my tongue. I feel so relieved in my dream that I am not slaughtered but poisoned. And then I wake up realizing I am on the street pavement, only dreaming. I feel even more relieved by the fact that I am alive.

Belgrade, Serbia, August 1995

This woman was one of the Krajina Serbs who fled their homes en masse after the collapse of the self-proclaimed republic in August 1995. Sickly thin and barefooted, she crouched in a corner near the entrance to the Belgrade fairgrounds, the central transport point for newly arrived refugees. She and her husband refused money or food. A woman from Belgrade approached, asking the whereabouts of her relatives. The two women stared at each other and started crying — they were old school chums. The barefooted woman refused to go to her friend's flat. No, she would wait for her son. Finally, someone offered cigarettes and both husband and wife were happy to accept one.

Woman, late 20s, Sarajevo

A LOVE LETTER

My darling, my only one,

A second month has gone by since I was torn from you, from our home, from our Sarajevo. I have learned in this short but for me so long time what sorrow, loneliness and nostalgia mean. And suffering, real suffering. My head is full of nightmares. I see scenes, as if watching a film. I love the two of us, our past happiness, our smiles, our walks. I still feel the warmth of your hands and the smell of

warm chestnuts, I still see the dear faces of our friends we kept
meeting wherever we went. Then suddenly the picture of our destroyed city appears, the sounds of shell, the sound of shots, shot,
shot. . . .

The police storm into our apartment, they search and take Mother
for questioning because my brother, who is a doctor, treats the
wounded who are on the "other" side. As if people who need help
don't live and get wounded there.

I see us crouched in the dark, cold cellar, where the beating of my
heart was only louder than the deafening noise of the explosions. I
see Dragana dead in a pink dress, as if sleeping. Her youth, destroyed by a bomb fragment, she was buried in the Big Park, the
park of her childhood. Days without electricity, water and food
follow. . . . Days of fear and disbelief of all that is happening. Then
I see our marriage. A modest war marriage. A marriage that many
did not like, because they could not understand how a Serbian
woman and a Muslim could get married. But there were friends
from both sides who in spite of everything honestly congratulated
us and were happy for us. I wished then that everyone would see us,
so that I could tell them how wrong they were, that I could cry out
how much, how infinitely I love you. To tell them how much I love
to be in your embrace, how warm and safe it is there.

How much I love your black, the blackest, the most beautiful eyes.
Is it possible that you would wish me evil because I am a Serbian
and you a Muslim? Should I because of that stop loving you? Should
I renounce you, you who have helped me dream, who have shown
me all the paths of love, even the most hidden, which I would never
have taken without you. Only you could have so slowly and patiently
removed all the barriers which guarded my vulnerable heart, only
you managed to completely penetrate my soul and to ultimately help
me to know and understand myself. I felt a great strength then; I
felt that the two of us, together, could do anything. There were no
barriers we could not overcome.

Suddenly in my mind there appears the pictures of us in prison in the former Officers' Club. Not even now do I know why they took us there. You stayed with me the whole night, although you could have left immediately. They did not like my name. Is it possible that only a name could be the criteria? No one will ever be able to convince me that only a name could be the criteria! No one will ever be able to convince me that there is any sense in dividing people in such a way. The only memory I have of that night is of trembling. I could not stop your hands, which embraced me firmly. Then I only remember the shelling and the ruins. I had a feeling that only Ciglane was being shelled. Then darkness and nightmares.

For nights and days I have been torturing myself to remember, to find out what happened that day. Terrible scenes pursue me in my dreams; I hear screams and someone's terrifying shriek. Terrified I open a door and wake up, tortured and wet with sweat. If only my dream would last longer, in order to see, to find out, maybe my nightmares would stop.

I know you cannot write much, but help me remember, give me a hint, give me a sign to destroy that terrible darkness in my head, which weighs upon me more than the most terrible truth. I must find out. I must find out what made you decide that I should hastily depart from the city. I know that you spent every moment with me, that you took care of me, protected me. I was as in a delirium, as in a trance. You never told me how you managed and how much you paid for me crossing the bridge. Then I was not capable of appreciating all the nice things we had in common and extracting energy from our union. Believe, believe firmly that we will see each other again; I wait for you. You know that I will always adhere to our "I love you, I want you and am in love with you."

Your wife

Belgrade, Serbia, 1993

The author is now in Canada. She is still waiting.

Dzevad, 29 years old, Srebrenica

LOVE LETTERS WHICH EVERYBODY READS

I worked for a long time in Belgrade and then I went to work in Russia when the war broke out. When I was in Russia I didn't even know if my family was alive. I went to the Red Cross in Belgrade but they refused to give any information. I had Serbian friends who stayed my friends and those who turned against me. Even people from Belgrade ran away from Belgrade, from the war, from the poverty, from the chaos. In November 1993, I came by plane to Vienna through Sofia: twice before the Hungarians made me go back because of my Bosnian passport.

I collected all the papers for my family to get out and the money too, but I don't know how they can pass all those borders and authorities. My wife is writing that there is a way through Belgrade if you pay, but in Belgrade nobody knows anything. I know that everything can be arranged for money, especially today in all these states who work without law, but the Austrians cannot understand that all authorities—Bosnian and Serbian—have to be bribed. I sent my family some papers but I will be nervous until they make it: those 110 kilometers could be fatal.

My wife is writing to me love letters, which everybody reads, thousands of them. I have been married for eight years, she is twenty-five, and we have two children. Here is one of her letters:

> How are you my love. Since I received three letters from you today, I am here with you immediately to tell you my news. First of all to ask you how are you, my love, and how is your life without the one who loves you most. We are alive and in good health and we wish to you the same. My love, I don't know how long we can live this way, how long this madness will last, but I can't stand it anymore. Sometimes I feel like killing myself. You cannot understand what my life is like: the children disobey me, they grow and I have no clothes for them so I have to use mine and mend them. Everything would be easier if you were with us, at least I could have somebody to talk to.

My beloved, you are the only one who can understand my suffering and my love which I keep only for you, my love, my love.

Your wife

If I knew that they will not be able to come here I would go back, leave all this and fight the war. But she is afraid of that. In Srebrenica there is no salt, people are getting all kinds of illnesses because of that. But only the very sick people can leave the city, probably because the war would seem useless if all the people left their homes. For me there is no life outside Bosnia, here dogs are more important than people. People here only run and work. We worked in Bosnia too, but we knew how to live. Here I run like them all the time, after trains, buses, papers . . . papers all the time . . .

When I first came to Vienna, I was in a camp for refugees. I was with a man from Croatia who was in the same room he was in during World War II. But they did not want to give me refugee status because I came from Russia and Serbia. I wanted to go back; I had nothing in Vienna like in Belgrade, but an order of nuns, the Carmelites, took me to their monastery and helped me with my papers. Their order is very strict; once they prohibited me even from talking to people, but then they said that they will dress me up as a nun if somebody comes to check on them. Even now they write letters of support for me when I feel desperate about my family and lonely. I haven't seen my wife for three years; I have only spoken to her a few times through the radio. Our voices were distorted.

Vienna, Austria, May 1995

Dzevad is a handsome man who lives in an upscale, well-equipped flat, earned through hard work. "All I do is work," he said, "and wait for my family to get out of Srebrenica." He explained that he was about to commit suicide a few months ago, when he had had no word from his wife, but some nuns from the convent saved him.

Thousands of refugees, mainly Muslims, crowded into Srebrenica throughout the war, leading to one of the greatest humanitarian disasters of the war. Heavy Serb shelling and road blockades kept humanitarian aid supplies away from the city for up to eleven months at a time. On May 6, 1993, the UN Security Council voted to make Srebrenica (along with Sarajevo, Tuzla, Zepa, Gorazde, and Bihac) safe havens. Serb forces were supposed to withdraw from these safe areas and allow access to humanitarian aid. This turned Srebrenica into a refugee holding cell. While aid trucks could get in with greater frequency, few humans could get out. Two months after Dzevad gave this interview, Serbs overran Srebrenica, forcing the approximately 50,000 residents on the road. According to survivors and human rights investigators, thousands of men were separated out, taken to detention camps, and shot and buried in mass graves. As far as we know, Dzevad's family is safe.

"The people here don't seem to understand that I don't WANT to be here."

"Were have three activities: eating, drinking, and smoking. . . . Oh, there is a fourth: waiting."

"It's best if we have problems. Then at least we can pass the time by trying to solve them. What's really bad is when we've solved everything."

Everyday refugee life bears no resemblance to everyday refugee dreams or fears. It is the opposite—a safe, slow death, away from the shellings, shielded from any emotions except for grief and the frustration of organizing a life around waiting. "Purgatory on earth," as more than one refugee has described her life in the decaying third-rate hotel, the abandoned workers' barracks, the wooden huts in the woods where young campers once played, the cramped room in the back of the home of a host family—relative, stranger, enemy, friend—alone or in the company of family or other refugees also struggling to survive. Even in these temporary nowhere places, refugees try to do more than merely survive; university professors and farmers alike attend language classes, learn how to knit, sell small objects on the streets, plant a small garden, enroll their children in school, squeak out a living that could lead to a future.

Once the joy of being alive and safe fades away, many refugees begin to question whether it was worthwhile. A woman compares her new home in a refugee camp to a beehive; another one considers herself invisible since she has no true contact with anybody; a man passes all his day sleeping, trying to forget the war, or watching the news, trying to remember it. "We are more than animals," says another woman; "we need more than food and a place to sleep." A poet writes, "I was broken, I was scattered, I was lost." This sense of displacement is most intense when refugees are forced far from their own cultures and given no opportunity to work in their new communities. Bosnian Muslims, a European people used to ski slopes in the winter and short shorts in the summer, are most miserable in the traditional Muslim land of Pakistan, despite their caretakers' hospitality. No amount of food, no soft mattress can compensate for being torn from home and placed in an utterly foreign land, a place where they will always be the most remote outsiders.

The few men among the refugee population often have the greatest difficulty adjusting. Women still maintain part of their earlier identity: they are still the caretakers, the ones looking after their children and older relatives, the ones cooking, mending, tending. They still find a way to make Turkish coffee (strong Nescafe can do in a pinch), to bake Bosnian bread on top of stoves, to make a birthday cake out of nothing. But the men whose identities are linked solely to their jobs outside the home have lost everything. Feeling useless and abandoned, and often secretly trying to cope with the humiliation and torture of prison camps, some men just end up becoming another burden to the women. One woman set down her washing long enough to look at her husband napping with their sons and remarked, "I used to have three children and now I have four."

Still, somehow women, men, and children do their best to keep living and to forget their past, at least until a letter from home, a phone call, the television news, forces its way into their refugee life.

Sena, 54 years old, Bosnia-Herzegovina
UNTITLED

As a glass
   a vase
      a window
         in winter
           I was broken

As leaves
   dust
      papers
         words
            I was scattered
In horizons
   in some clouds
      strange
         useless
            I was lost.

Belgrade, Serbia, 1995

Sena writes poetry with the scent of Herzegovina and colors of the valley of the Neretva River, a land she lived in her entire life — that is, before war. She lives in a refugee camp near Belgrade and hopes to return.

Ademir Karisik, 21 years old, Sarajevo

PAKISTAN

Built a fire
Thousands of miles away
To light my long way home
I ride a comet
My tail is long to stay
Silence is a heavy stone
I fight the world and take all they can give
There are times my heart hangs low
Born to walk against the wind
Born to hear my name
No matter where I stand
I'm alone.

Islamabad, Pakistan, August 1994

Working as a translator and assistant for the Bosnian government, Ademir accompanied the Bosnian refugees who traveled from Croatia to Pakistan in the spring of 1993. Once in Pakistan, Ademir became a refugee himself, as he did not have the necessary documents to get out once he had entered. Ademir was one of the main leaders in the Hajji complex — the place where Bosnians were housed near Islamabad. He helped numerous fellow Bosnians leave for other countries and was instrumental in setting up an education system in the camp. While he refused to tell his story, he quietly submitted this poem, which belies his tough facade.

In the winter of 1995, Ademir left for Turkey, en route to his beloved Sarajevo. The other refugees from Pakistan have not heard from him since then. Rumor has it that he made it to Sarajevo.

S., 40s, Sarajevo

LETTER

I got a letter from a friend of mine in Sarajevo. It was about graves. A lot of people without arms, legs, eyes. I walked all day through the streets here looking for vegetables but I couldn't buy anything. I was thinking about those graves, those arms and legs. I don't know what people saw when they looked at my face because I wasn't there.

Berlin, Germany, 1994

This letter was sent by a peace worker from Germany; she had received it from a woman refugee. Both wish to remain anonymous.

Man, 60 years old, Sarajevo
LETTER TO MY DAUGHTERS

Sarajevo, 27 January 1993

My dearest daughters,

Everything is emptied. I want to tell you: my veins have been emptied, my arteries, my kidneys, my brains, my heart. Everything, but what I am afraid most is that my soul has become completely empty.

I am sorry but I have to tell you really cruel things, to tell you about my friends whom I lost, who have been killed: the painter Rizovic, Cindric, Zoran Bajbutovic, Vesna Bugarski, Alija Kucukalic (him a long time ago).

And then there are all those who are alive, but half alive.

They tell me I have to live, and I am listening to them, but I am not able to do it.

My loves, my girls, I am sorry. You shouldn't be angry with your daddy because he has become so EMPTY. Completely EMPTY.

I feel like an actor without an audience.

> ". . . We thought we flew
> And instead we fell on the ground.
> Suddenly
> Everything exploded around us."

But one thing I have to tell you: that I love you very, very, very much and that the only thing about me that doesn't make me unhappy is that you two exist, your mother and poor Bessy.

With great love your
Daddy

This letter was written by an architect to his two daughters, refugees in Milan. His daughters received the letter at the beginning of March 1993, after they had learned of his death in Sarajevo on January 29, 1993. The letter was originally published in Anna Cataldi, ed., Sarajevo: Voci da un assedio (Milano: Baldina and Castoldi, 1993).

This letter was written more than nine months after the onset of the siege of Sarajevo. Although Sarajevo was under shelling and sniper fire for much longer, what is known as the "siege of Sarajevo" lasted from April 5, 1992, to August 1993.

Hvalenka Carrara, early 30s, Croatia

ALMEDIN KILLS GHOSTS

A day like any other.

We get up in the morning, we prepare breakfast, we eat, we laugh; we play with the kitten, a little tramp arrived from who knows where. The kitten is still fearful; he hides away. "Maybe he is also a refugee?" asks my son. We laugh and we continue to play with our little tramp. The children are eating breakfast and watching the cartoons, but only for five minutes because we have to leave soon. He to the day care and Ivona, "my" other child, to her school. Ivona arrived from Bosnia almost a year ago. Alone. Her mother and father stayed behind. She is seven years old, and she began school here. She is the best in her class, and she has already made many friends. Her mother arrived three months ago and is now waiting for school to end. Then, they'll see what to do.

After I finish everything, I rush to work. This time to translate for a group of psychotherapists. We find ourselves in a refugee camp in Zagreb. We enter barracks number six. There is little room, one can hardly enter because it's so crowded with beds. Samira, the mother, is making a kind of pie, "pita," the Bosnian specialty. We ask her if we could talk to her and to the children. She leaves everything and goes to call for the two that are playing outside. She has four daughters and one boy. Almedin, the youngest, is six years old. He immediately agreed to speak with us, but his answers are short.

Here they are alone; some of the family is in Spain and some are at another refugee camp here in Zagreb.

Almedin is lively, we talk to him for a little while. He sings the songs he learned in the camp's day care for us. He makes us listen to a song about flowers and says that it's the song his mother likes the most. He is happy at the camp, he is learning a lot of things, and he can play. His mother is listening to him while she prepares the pita and puts it in the oven to bake. She says, "Who taught you the names of the flowers when we lived in Bosnia?" He does not answer, pretends not to hear, starts to count to twenty. Samira tells us: "It was his grandpa who taught him so many things. The boy was very attached to him . . . and now Grandpa is gone." She continues to speak: "We were seated, just as we are now, and we were doing the usual things. All of a sudden they entered and forced all the men out: my husband, his brother and Grandpa. We were waiting without even trying to see what was happening. Later, it was all over . . ." She stops talking abruptly, doesn't move, she remains seated on the bed, looking like she is not aware of our presence. The oldest daughter, of seventeen, does not say anything and is standing still. A beautiful girl, with dark hair and blue eyes. Only Almedin is trying to call attention to himself. He pops out of his hole under the sheets on the bed. "I'm a king, I'm the greatest of all of you!" Then he stops fast, the role of the greatest does not impress him much.

Samira picks up on her story: "Four hours later, my daughter went to search for her father without me knowing. It was she who found them. Dead. All. All the men from the village. My son is not a man yet. I have feared for him, because among the others killed there were also some boys—fourteen, fifteen years old—they were only children . . ." She speaks without stopping, but with a dreary, even voice, a voice that makes chills go up your back. Her voice is there, but yet silence has filled the room. Almedin starts to cry. He is asking for something from his mother that she does not want to give him. He insists, and finally she surrenders: it is a toy pistol. Almedin takes it and goes out. He goes to fight with who knows what enemy. Maybe it is the only thing that he can do to kill the ghosts.

We ask, "Is anybody angry about everything that happened?"

"Yes, of course!" But there is no aggression, no passion.

"After all, maybe it's only destiny," adds Samira. But there is no anger against destiny either.

"These things should not happen to anybody, no person deserves it, everybody has children. The children are left alone and cannot carry all of that horror within them."

The silence again.

"There is one thing I can never forgive. They did not bury the murdered, the bodies stayed there. We covered the dead with sheets, but they did not allow us to bury the bodies. We should have insisted, but we, the women, were afraid for our children. They could have killed us as well, and the children would have been left completely alone. But we should have insisted anyway. I will never forgive myself . . ." She stops and she starts to cry. Finally, a little bit of her self shows. But it is an empty self. Samira is bearing alone all the anger that should have been directed against somebody else, to those who have done so much evil.

The crying ends quickly.

We talk to the oldest daughter. We ask her what she would like in the future. A moment of silence, and then she says: "Peace." Peace is the only thing that she can imagine. A future does not exist, until there is peace. Something concrete has to happen in order for one to be able to start thinking again, to be able to exist again. The impulse to start living has to come from the outside, because there is little energy left in them. In this situation without a future, in this situation of a nonlife, it is impossible to change anything.

"What do you miss from the past?"

"My father."

That's all, there is nothing after that. She is seventeen years old, it's the time for her to fall in love, to laugh with her friends. Besides, she is so beautiful.

We ask about the other daughters: "Do they go to school?"

"No, I cannot afford that now. The books, the textbooks . . . No, how could I afford it?" Maybe that is not the real reason, maybe it's only the need for having the children near her, I think.

A girl, eight years old, comes in with a friend. I recognize her. It is the girl that I met when we arrived here for the first time, five months ago. It's she who is always beside us, lively, happy. She has become a real aid: in the day care, she assists the teachers and she puts the toys in order for the youngest children, always with a smile on her face. I am surprised to see her, I didn't realize that this was her family. She is calm now, she is listening seriously and smiling shyly. Afterward, she talks in a soft voice to her friend. She stays a little bit with us, and then leaves.

The conversation with her mother becomes more difficult, the answers shorter and shorter. I have the impression that we are annoying her. I ask her if she plans to join the rest of the family in Spain.

"Yes, maybe."

"Wouldn't it be difficult now to learn a new language, to find oneself among strangers?"

"Difficult? No. Why would it be? Here or at another place, what's the difference? We don't belong in this place, and not anywhere else either. In the end, the only thing I really want is to return to Bosnia. I know everything is burned there, that nothing is left. But I want to return there. Only there."

We prepare ourselves to leave, feeling emptiness inside. We don't find the words to tell her good-bye. One of us asks her if she has a message for the people abroad. Surprised by the question, she answers: "No, nobody would understand anyway."

I make a sign to her that the pita is burning. She says: "Oh, I see . . ." and stands up slowly to get it out of the oven. Without alarm. I believe that even if the barracks were on fire she would have said with calmness, "Oh, I see . . ."

We finish drinking the coffee that she offered. We enjoy it as you do in Bosnia, with a piece of sugar. She looks at us, for the first time a smile lights up her face: "I have made the sugar. I used to make it at home always . . ." We leave her. The smile still lights her face. She is happy to be able to offer us the coffee: it is a gesture that takes her home.

It is cold outside, the girl of eight is playing, lively as always; she approaches us with the smile of an accomplice and says, "You are leaving now?"

Almedin has still not returned: he is killing ghosts someplace. It is evening, the time has come for us to go. I pass again down the same road: the children are running, the elderly are seated on benches, the days are longer, and the sand bags are still at the windows.

Zagreb, Croatia, 1994

The author is a Croat of Italian ancestry. She is fluent in both Italian and Croatian. While not a refugee herself, she has been working in refugee camps in Croatia as a translator for therapists and journalists. The camp she describes is one of many in the Zagreb environs.

A DAY IN THE LIFE

One of the most difficult exercises for refugees anywhere is to compare one day of their life as a refugee to one ordinary day in their past. Putting pencil to paper, the refugees are forced to remember the simple rhythm of life that they've left behind. Below are two "day in the life" comparisons, by Hajrija Cemer and her husband, Muriz, who at the time of this writing were at the Hajji complex in Pakistan.

Hajrija Cemer, late 30s, Donji Vakuf

ONE DAY IN DONJI VAKUF

Friday, February 23, 1990
6:10 A.M.: I wake up, go to the bathroom, and prepare myself for work. After that I go to the kitchen and make breakfast for my

family. I eat my breakfast and set the table for the rest of them. I leave a message for my husband: "On your way back from school buy bread, milk, meat; your lunch is in the fridge—soup and cabbage rolls. Dessert is in the cupboard." Before I leave for work, I wake up my husband.

6:45 A.M.: I leave my home.

6:55 A.M.: I am in my office and I prepare myself for the working day ahead. First thing is a morning coffee and chatting about everyday happenings, such as children, shopping, increase of prices.

11:30 A.M.: During the lunch break I go to the rear office to see my friend. We talk about going out somewhere in the evening.

12:00 NOON: I return to my office and continue to work.

3:00 P.M.: Working hours are finished and I leave. I wait for my colleague and we chat on our way home.

3:20 P.M.: I am at home. My children are playing football. I enter the front yard and they come into the house with me. They tell me about their day in school and go in the study to do their homework. I start with my everyday obligations—washing dishes, laundry, dusting.

6:30 P.M.: My husband and I are going out for our usual walk, in the city walking area. We meet our friends, go with them to the cafe, and discuss our plans for going on a ski weekend (in Rostovo, 16 kilometers away).

9:00 P.M.: I come home and see my children watching TV. I prepare things for tomorrow's ski weekend.

10:00 P.M.: The children go to sleep, and I stay up to finish what's left that has to be done in the house.

ANY DAY IN PAKISTAN

8:00 A.M.: I get up and go to the bathroom. After that I enter the kitchen to make bread and breakfast.

11:00 A.M.: The children wake up, eat and go outside. I make up the beds, clean the room, kitchen and the bathroom.

1:00 P.M.: I make lunch and we eat. I wash dishes and after that, exhausted, I go to the bathroom to do the laundry by hand. Everything is finished by 5:00 P.M. and I take a shower and lay down to rest for a while.

7:00 P.M.: I have an afternoon coffee with my husband and we talk about the expiring day, our possible departure and remember all those beautiful days in Bosnia.

8:00 P.M.: My husband and I go outside for a walk in the camp. We make two circles around the camp's wall.

9:00 P.M.: My husband goes to listen to the news and I go to see my friend in front of pavilion number four. We talk until early in the morning about going away from Pakistan.

Muriz Cemer, early 40s, Donji Vakuf

ONE DAY IN DONJI VAKUF

Friday, February 23, 1990

6:45 A.M.: My wife wakes up the children and me and she leaves for work. I am still in bed while the children are going to the bathroom and dressing. After the children have their turn, I go to the bathroom and shave.

7:10 A.M.: We are all dressed and ready. The table has already been set by my wife, so we sit and have breakfast. While eating, we talk about the coming day and make plans for it.

7:30 A.M.: We finish breakfast. The children check the inside of their school bags and we leave home. On my way to work I buy the daily news. My children join other kids who are on their way to school.

7:45 A.M.: I have my first morning coffee in the room for the teaching staff and I also read newspapers.

7:55 A.M.: I take the class register and go to my office and after that to the gym to start my class.

12:10 P.M.: I finish with classes and return to my office. I go through my paperwork.

1:00 P.M.: I leave school.

1:15 P.M.: I come home and my children are already there. I warm up the lunch my wife made the previous evening and set up the table. My children and I are eating and talking about their day at school.

2:00 P.M.: I clean the table and go to the cellar to turn on the central heating. The children are in the front yard, playing football.

3:20 P.M.: My wife comes back from work. The children come into the house and begin their homework. I read daily and weekly newspapers and after that some professional literature to prepare myself for advanced classes.

5:00 P.M.: I go to the garage and make some small repairs.

6:30 P.M.: My wife and I go for our usual walk, then to a cafe to meet some friends.

9:00 P.M.: We are back at home. I check on my children's homework. Then, we eat some dinner. I go to the cellar and check on the central heating. After that, I pack our ski outfits together with my children's.

10:00 P.M.: The children go to bed. I watch TV, wait for the news and weather forecast.

11:00–11:30 P.M.: I go to bed.

ANY DAY IN PAKISTAN

11:00 A.M.: I get up.

11:20 A.M.: I am going to the post office.

12:00 NOON: I am talking to other people in front of the pavilion.

1:00–2:00 P.M.: I am having lunch.

3:00 P.M.: I am writing a letter.

4:30 P.M.: I am sleeping.

7:00 P.M.: I am having coffee.

8:00 P.M.: I am going for a walk.

9:00 P.M.: I am listening to the news.

10:00 P.M.: I am listening to the news.

12:00 MIDNIGHT: I am listening to the news.

1:00 A.M.: I am listening to the news.

Islamabad, Pakistan, August 1995

Hajrija and Muriz met over a dozen years ago, when Muriz was a dashing young physical education teacher and Hajrija was a secondary school student. Shortly after her graduation, they married. They now have two sons and are still deeply in love. The war began in their hometown, Donji Vakuf, when Serb forces bombed a bridge in the middle of town. This couple's son was the last boy to ride his bike over the bridge before it blew up.

Hajrija and Muriz wrote these descriptions as part of the writing workshops conducted by Julie Mertus and Eve Ensler in refugee camps in Pakistan. At the time, both Hajrija and Muriz appeared very sad and exhausted. They had been waiting nearly a year for visas to the United States. Muriz was especially eager to hear about the weather in Utica, N.Y., their planned destination. Was it cold like Bosnia? Could they ski? Would the boys do well in school? The family made it to Utica in the spring of 1995. Bosnians retook Donji Vakuf in the fall of 1995, and as of this writing Hajrija and Muriz are considering returning home.

Naser, late 30s, Donji Vakuf

FROM PAKISTAN TO NEW YORK

Your letter brings in my dark life a little light. Never mind that you are thousands of kilometers away. We have a hard life here, and every day someone is leaving us. We feel that we are forgotten by everyone. Step by step, people are going to other countries; only we wait to see America. . . .

I'm so tired from everything that has happened to me, to my innocent people and to my country. The last three years were so hard for me, with many difficult moments. I think a normal man can't stand this situation.

My pain I can write only to you, and we miss you a lot.

My only wish in life is to help my children and to see once more the sky and sun in my country.

Please one night, take two glasses, one for you and one for me, drink and think about me as a man, a man who loved to live but other people didn't give him the chance to live. . . .

I will wait and try to stand up from the ashes.

Islamabad, Pakistan, November 1994

Naser, one of the Bosnians who was a refugee in Pakistan, lost ten members of his family in the war, including all of his brothers, his father, and his father-in-law. After the war began in his hometown, Donji Vakuf, Naser brought his family to safety, but his father refused to leave, believing that his reputation would protect him. Naser soon lost contact with his father and other male relatives. He later learned that Serb forces had imprisoned and tortured them to death in the local police headquarters, less than a mile from his home. "I would go each day to the woods by Donji Vakuf, the place where the men were escaping to, and I would ask everyone about my father," Naser remembered. "No one would tell me anything. But then finally someone said he was dead."

Naser brought his family to the Dalmatian Coast in Croatia, but he returned to Bosnia to work on humanitarian aid projects. During one of his trips to visit his family, the Croatia-Bosnia border was sealed. Naser just happened to be in Croatia when Croatian authorities gave his family twenty-four hours to leave the country.

Despite his great pain, Naser still has an amazing sense of humor and, somehow, the will to survive. He now lives with his family in Utica, N.Y., where he has become a leader of Bosnian refugees there.

Elderly man and woman in their 70s, a village near Foca

UNTITLED

Two steps down into a squalid basement room, an elderly man and woman lie together on dusty gray mats in the center of a small square room. The air is thick from the smoke of the wood stove; the single window is sealed shut. "They are hiding from the authorities," the refugee worker says. "These people saw terrible things." They are too afraid to declare themselves refugees. Bins of flour, salt, sugar, a large can of oil, a tin of powdered milk — donations from the underground Muslim charity — line a low wooden shelf. "But she can't really stand, can't really cook." The refugee worker greets the old woman with a yell. "She can't hear well." He pauses and looks around the room. "We have a real problem here."

MAN: I had two cows and thirteen chickens. When they came for us, I hid under the bridge. I can't even tell you what I saw. I cry every night because of what I saw.

They found me under the bridge. One of them put a gun inside my mouth. I told him to shoot me, but one of them, my neighbor, told him to stop. The one who had the gun pushed me onto my knees. My neighbor told me to leave.

WOMAN: Look at my legs! The refugee camp in Hungary was hell. Hell. I fell down and broke my leg, see! I have pain.

MAN: We went to Hungary because someone put us in a bus and took us there. But we didn't want to be there. We didn't like it there. It wasn't our country.

WOMAN: They didn't help me at all. Can you see my legs?

MAN: When she fell, they wouldn't give her an operation. They gave her a stick, that's all. We were garbage.

WOMAN: (Showing tattered remains of documents) Look, I was a refugee! I had these! And this doesn't help me.

MAN: I didn't like being outside my country. I was never a Turk. I was a Yugoslav. I was Muslim and Yugoslav. We are too old to be outside our country.

An Albanian came to the hostel where we were staying. He was a worker. He could see what was going on. He told us that we could come with him to Kosovo if we wanted to. Anything was better than that place. We didn't have any of the right papers at the border, but he told the guards that we were just his relatives. We didn't say anything and they let us pass into Serbia and we came here. He told us that there were Muslims here and they could take care of us. We came here.

WOMAN: My leg hurts. I have bad dreams too.

MAN: They bring us things to eat but that is not what we want. I can tell you one thing. If you really wanted to help me, you would shoot me right now and put me out of my misery.

Pristina, Kosovo, February 1994

According to Merhamet, the Muslim humanitarian aid group (which the Serbian regime has banned from Kosovo and which operates clandestinely), hundreds of Bosnian Muslim refugees live "illegally" in Kosovo, the troubled southern part of reduced Yugoslavia, which is 90 percent ethnic Albanian. "Most of them," a Merhamet volunteer explains, "don't want to be here. Most of them were trying to get into Macedonia but they couldn't get across the border." The Bosnian Muslims in Kosovo are extremely afraid, as they are a minority within a minority — Muslims in a Serbian-controlled state and Bosnians in an Albanian-populated society (where Albanians practice both Muslim and Catholic faiths). To date, Albanians have been the primary group to come to the aid of Bosnian Muslims in Kosovo. UNHCR

does not provide aid for these refugees (as they are not "officially registered").
For the most part, Bosnian Muslims in Kosovo subsist on donations from
Mother Teresa, from the Albanian-run humanitarian aid group, and to a
lesser extent from the few international groups working in Kosovo, such as
Mercy Corps International. But most international groups dismiss the Bos-
nian Muslim population as being "numerically insignificant" or "impossible
to find" (answers given by such groups repeatedly to the editors).

The couple interviewed here come from a region where Serb forces suc-
cessfully killed or pushed out nearly all Muslim residents.

Mirjana Nuspahic, Bosanski Brod

FROM DAY TO DAY

You cannot help thinking about this refugee life, here in the valley.
Even now, as I lie in my bed and listen to the change of guards on
the other side of the wire, I look at the dim and distant Moon. Ein-
stein once said that everything is relative except absolute zero, so
now I think: what are we, the one or the other? Here, with us,
everything has been calculated, everybody knows what is going to
happen and when. Breakfast, lunch, dinner. The walk around the
polygon. Leaving for the town. Driving one crazy. From day to day,
from month to month. Sometimes, the wind chases us back into
these edifices of sorrow. Occasionally, when I think I won't hold
much longer, I get out of this madhouse, but then I fly into the
circular flow of my thoughts that had remained inside. And cease-
lessly the same route, the same building, it seems that even the
people are the same. Those who live here look like machines that
need only fuel to run, like living dolls—they feed in order to survive. No one can reach their psyche. Five psychiatrists could once
again defend their doctoral dissertation working on each and every
individual.

Everybody always says the same things, it is only the audience that
changes. Their faces mirror envy, jealousy, aggressiveness, nervous-

ness, terror. More or less, depending on the person. In most cases their lives are the same. As good old Balasevic (a pop singer) says: "The principle is the same, the rest are nuances!" When I take my body for a walk and come back, the first thing that pierces my eyes is a sticker made of tin that says everything. As I approach these huge buildings, similar to three beehives where a confusion is boiling as it nears the explosion, my eyes, my nose, my ears fill with the cries of a child and shrill shrieks of its mother who quarrels about the child's broken nose, while quite accidentally she has forgotten her coffee and her cigarettes and is not even aware that she is standing outside—the stench of the same food spreading from the garbage cans, thrown almost directly from the kitchen. On every window there hangs sad, freshly washed underwear, as if it knew it doesn't belong here; the noise from the megaphones constantly makes people joyful or sad. Two or three things caught in a glimpse are enough to comprehend the sort of life these people lead.

And while the night passes slowly, the polygon becomes deserted; only the strong wind scatters the leaves, the paper casually thrown away, empty beer cans and other rubbish. In the morning, when the beehive wakes again, new coffees, clouds of cigarette smoke, pies and an occasional cookie, dirty children and cries from the women who clean will liven up this piece of dismembered Bosnia, put together even here. And then again and again and again. From day to day.

Bosanski Brod, a city in northern Bosnia on the border with Croatia, saw fighting between Bosnians (mainly Muslims) and Croats, and then between Bosnians and Serbs. In October 1992, Croatian President Tudjman ordered Bosnian Croat troops out of Bosanski Brod, opening the way for Serb forces to take the city. Refugees from Bosanski Brod went north, through Croatia to Slovenia, and often to further destinations north and west. This essay was written for the magazine Izi: Refugees for Refugees, *published by a group run by refugees in Ljubljana, Slovenia.*

V., 29 years old, northern Bosnia-Herzegovina

LUXURY BANANAS

My husband and I are doctors; we both studied medicine in Bosnia. Before the war, we had friends from everywhere, all over Yugoslavia. We got married about a year before the war. I gave birth to a son in November, seven months after the war began. When fighting began in Bosnia in the spring of 1992, my husband was fired and I was told to go on leave. There was enormous inflation and we couldn't even buy a box of matches with our pay, if we got it at all.

My husband's father was a barber and he had to close his shop. In the mornings, he would find all of his windows smashed. He tried putting wood on the windows but then someone would get into the store and destroy everything. We were very afraid because there was a lot of ethnic cleansing. There were a lot of us living in the same house: my baby and myself, my husband and his parents, brothers and sisters. My grandmother then came to live with my mother, because her part of town was burned and no houses were left. Somehow we managed to survive.

It was complete chaos. No one knew the best thing to do. I didn't know whether I could trust my old friends. I couldn't rely on anyone and I had to look after my son. We decided to join a convoy to Croatia. We didn't even believe that the convoy would make it because we had lost trust in everyone and didn't believe anything. We had to pay six hundred German marks for the convoy. This was a fortune for us: it meant that we might be saved, but it also meant that our family would be left with almost nothing. Our family could feed themselves for six months on three hundred marks. They told us to take it and go.

We couldn't find any work in Zagreb, so we tried living in several smaller towns and villages. We moved around, doing everything just to earn some money. I remembered reading E. M. Remarque's novels about Jewish refugees before the Second World War really began. I was like them. I was selling cosmetics, washing hallways, milking cows, cleaning stables—things I had never done before in my life. I was surprised how quickly I could learn. I was forced to obey people who were trying to humiliate me as if I had chosen to be there, as if I wanted to be a beggar, as if I asked for the life of a refugee. Many times I regretted that I didn't know any handicraft— that I was not a seamstress, hairdresser, or something else that I could do with my hands and not with my head, because no one wanted doctors (especially Muslims). My husband was in the same position. He had to do the worst physical jobs and they paid very poorly.

It took me a whole year of refugee life before I could afford to buy bananas for my child. Luxury bananas. Whenever I buy something like that we feel like we are having a party.

I was in contact with a friend of mine from Belgrade during all of this time. Mail doesn't go from my city in Bosnia to Zagreb, or from Zagreb to my city, but it now it goes in both directions to Belgrade. Ever since mail opened up again between Zagreb and Belgrade, my mother and I have communicated by sending letters to my friend in Belgrade, who in turn posts them on to us. Two months ago, my mother sent all of my own and my husband's important personal documents and photographs through this friend. We had left everything (birth certificates, diplomas, licenses) behind.

Zagreb, Croatia, February 1995

V. wishes to remain anonymous out of fear of retribution. V. now lives with her husband and child in the United States. Both V. and her husband work for six dollars an hour in a factory; there is little hope of medical school. They don't have much time to talk to people at her workplace, so they do not even learn English on the job. "Here people work all the time and sleep," complained V. "There's no community like in Bosnia. I suppose it might be better for people if they have education and money." The family hopes to go back to Bosnia.

V. sent any money she could save home to her mother. In the fall of 1995,

Serbs forced V.'s mother to leave her town. She had to walk on a difficult trail for over two days, carrying her mother-in-law on her back. V.'s mother died a week after she completed her exodus march.

Anonymous, Bosnia-Herzegovina

INVISIBLE

I came to Switzerland for medical treatment, but I cannot tell you the details because I can't let anyone know I'm still here. My stay was supposed to be temporary. I was supposed to have the operation and then return back to my city. One relative was allowed to accompany me here. After the operation, they gave me some time to recover, to make sure that I had no complications.

I met some other people who were in the same situation as me. We were all nothing. Not refugees. Not a part of Switzerland or Bosnia. Nothing. I was very worried all the time about what was happening in Bosnia, what was happening to my family, what would happen to them, whether I would ever see them again. All black things were coming into my mind. I felt bad that I was here and safe when my family was in danger and I never knew what the next day would bring. I knew I was one of the lucky ones who had this special treatment but I would have been more than happy to trade my fortune with my family.

And all during this time I was supposed to recover my health. I couldn't eat, I couldn't sleep, and I couldn't get better. I was so weak.

The people who brought us here and all of the Swiss doctors were so nice to us. Their only goal was to take care of us and to make us better. Fortunately, I knew German. I became very close to one doctor who helped me. She knew that I was still sick, so she refused to send me back to Bosnia. One day, I kept my appointment with the doctor and then never went back. I've tried to make myself invisible.

I don't know how to write how I feel. I don't have the words.

I am trying to survive here but this is not my place. I don't fit in here. I can see people looking at me when I walk down the street. No one says anything bad. They don't say anything nice either. Maybe they don't see me. Maybe I am just another foreigner who can pick up their garbage.

I miss having coffee with my friends. I miss seeing people who know me.

What is a typical day like for me? It is a day of waiting. Uncertainty. Physical and mental pain. I miss seeing people who know me. I rely on the kindness of some people around me who make sure I have enough to eat and that I have a place to stay. A refugee is a human being. I am more of an animal, and some days I think I am worse because it seems that in Switzerland animals are treated much better than foreigners.

Switzerland, February 1995

Switzerland was one of several countries that treated injured civilians from Bosnia-Herzegovina. This is not the only patient who decided to prolong a medical stay, nor is Switzerland the only country with patients turned "illegal refugees."

S., 54 years old, Doboj
UNWANTED

I try to read the German newspapers as infrequently as possible now, but every once in a while I buy one and take a look. There are so many stories about how Germany is flooded with refugees, especially those refugees from Bosnia. I read about why we are a danger, why we should be kept out. Meanwhile, I, the one with the college education, take care of their children and clean their houses. Never before in my life did I ever step foot anywhere where I was not wanted. I do not recognize what I have become.

None of us have legal papers. We came too late. They already had enough of us refugees. But we are the ones who stayed so long because we never wanted to come. We are the ones who came only after we lost family members, only after our houses and towns had become completely destroyed. I don't know what I would say if I met the man who wrote in the paper that we are mostly economic migrants. What does he know about my life? Should I show him the photos? No, he doesn't deserve to know me.

Germany, February 1995

Germany has one of the largest numbers of both legal and "illegal" refugees from Croatia and Bosnia-Herzegovina. Many of these refugees have relatives or friends who had arrived before the war, often as guest workers. This refugee came in search of work, after a stay in Croatia and Hungary.

Fikreta, 36 years old, Mali Zvornik

THE LAW BREAKERS

My city is now in Serbian hands, "ethnically clean." I am a Muslim. After the outbreak of war, after the cleansing, the killing of children, I came to Mali Zvornik, then to Belgrade where I had some friends. In Belgrade I got a passport, but I couldn't go anywhere outside with that passport. My brothers escaped from the war and went to Austria and Germany. I was alone with my seventy-year-old mother.

Law made me break the law. We bought some false Slovenian passports, which needed no visas, for two thousand German marks each. They caught us at the Hungarian border and held us for fifteen days; we had to pay for everything, for the stay in a prison, even for the transport. They kept us in this prison with bars on the windows. They called it a military barrack, and afterwards they took us to a center for refugees from all countries.

Then we came here to this Red Cross center in Budapest. It is nice here; it is calm and clean. But I suffer because I broke the law. But it wasn't our fault. We would have all liked to stay in our places, our homes with our families, clean.

Now I am waiting for a Bosnian passport to become legal in order to go to Germany and work. In Serbia nobody disturbed me, but I could not work because I was from Zvornik and they would have taken me back there to work. I watched over the river Drina as my house was torn down to the earth, bit by bit; it was robbed, but I didn't dare cross that river. Only Serbs could live there, even though nobody really said you must go. Many uniforms have attacked Zvornik. I was not in any party and I am the victim of this status, someone who didn't have quick reactions.

Once Zvornik was mainly Muslim. The Serbs went out first and we were all surprised, but we soon realized that it was a test. They were told to go. I wasn't afraid but when I heard on the radio that Zvornik was being attacked, all friendships broke up, people divided themselves. When the shooting started I didn't even know who was shooting, I only tried to stay alive. Then the grenades came, and we spent time in the cellars, lots of us. Then various armies came, one after another: Arkan's Seselj's, the army. Some people were taken for exchange but then seized by another army and killed immediately or after walking ten meters. They told us to go to Serbia, but then they called us all to come back, whatever our nationality. But they had already started to cleanse the city and the villages, to persecute and kill Muslims if they found them at home. They would bring buses full of Serbians to populate the villages held by Muslims. It was all very near, it was madness; the best thing was to run away somewhere. I had to take care of my mother because everyone else had left.

I am not thinking of going back to Bosnia, even if it is my country. Zvornik is the Serbian corridor and I don't want to be a refugee in my own country. Here we are of all nationalities and we get along together, we speak about the causes of the war and we are very happy to be able to use our native language.

All of us who were caught entering Hungary illegally were together in the same center: those who used drugs, those who killed, and those of us who were saving our lives. In the camp there were not even doors, only partitions, and we were all together. It was a terrible place; I didn't know how to explain some things to my mother. She is too old to understand, to change, to drop her old habits.

A young woman with a five-month-old baby tried five times to cross the border illegally. The last time three policemen took her to buy milk for the baby. She entered the shop and never came out. Since she has been missing for some time, I hope she did finally manage to escape.

On the Hungarian border where there is a camp for Bosnian refugees, there are two cafes, one visited by Serbs, one by Bosnians. When they get drunk, since the places are very close to each other, they sing in the dark together and laugh and cry . . . that really touches me deeply.

Budapest, June 1995

Officials at the Budpest Red Cross were very helpful in organizing meetings with refugees. Fikreta told her story into a tape recorder in the Red Cross dining room. She longed for her lost home, but she also had great curiosity about her future. She was anxious, as if she were reading a book and had yet to hear the ending. Within a month after telling this story, Fikreta made it to Germany.

Jadranka P., 34 years old, Trebinje

TOMORROW IS ANOTHER DAY

My name is Jadranka P. I was born in 1960 in Trebinje (Herzegovina) and I graduated in political science from the University of Sarajevo. We were all friends; I miss them so much, I want to meet them and tell them I am still the same.

Myself and my two sons (born 1987, 1988) left Sarajevo April 2, 1992, just two days before the war started. My husband told me in those days: "Take the children and go to Belgrade. There are rumors there will be war here." I didn't believe it; I refused to go, but when my girlfriend left with her children, I left too.

When we arrived in Belgrade we first stayed at my father-in-law and his wife's home. He used to visit us often in Sarajevo; we always welcomed him. My husband is his only son: my children are his only grandsons. We escaped because of the war, not for pleasure. We didn't want to disturb anybody. But my mother-in-law was not kind at all. She didn't even try to hide her unkindness. I approached her as an enemy. I had only one suitcase.

Then the first bad sign appeared: my younger son began to cough. He had been in the hospital many times in Sarajevo because of his bronchitis. He had to go to the hospital in Belgrade too, but without me. And there the drama begins. He screamed and cried. . . . A friendly doctor agreed to see him, his big shining eyes are permanently in my mind.

As always bad things come one after another, so my father-in-law and his wife started to quarrel with me. They wanted me to live by their very strange rules; they wanted to know everything: why do I go somewhere, where do I go, why I don't do something the way they do. I tried not to answer their provocative questions. I smoked a lot of cigarettes, drank too much coffee, cried when nobody was around, and I made a decision to go back to Sarajevo. I took my son out of the hospital and tried to phone my husband, but the lines were down: in Sarajevo a real horrible war had begun. What had happened to my husband?

The doctors explained to me that my son's sense of hearing was damaged by the oxygen in his incubator. I had to find a special instrument for his ears but I had no job, no money, no home, I am a refugee. To make matters worse, my husband's father and his wife kicked us out. They said they needed silence and order and we made their everyday life impossible. Where could we possibly go?

I have an old nice aunt in Pancevo, a small town about twenty kilometers from Belgrade. We went to her. Although she's seventy-two and has a small uncomfortable flat, she was happy to see us.

So we started again. Every morning now we go to Belgrade by bus, to the hospital with my sick son, we come back some hours later, then I prepare lunch, wash clothes, clean the flat, try to be patient with my sons even when they are nervous and restless. . . . I've already lost ten kilos of my weight and my son must go to the hospital again.

I write from the hospital. There is a wing of that old, gray house that has been restored a bit for refugee women with children. My son is under the doctor's control in a room a couple meters away from us. It is very crowded, there are many people in one room, everybody has their own trouble and pain, and there can't be the kind of order that we used to have in our homes. But, this is a refugee's life: Tomorrow is another day.

Belgrade, Serbia, 1994

After she wrote this story, Jadranka's son went blind. Still, Jadranka always is in high spirits, joking constantly about her life. In her own dark humor, she tells people that she can't go abroad because no country wants her with a sick child. Jadranka is still separated from her husband.

Behka Granov (born Mulahmetovic), Foca

HOW I MANAGED TO SURVIVE

For the first time in twenty months, thanks to the ham radio, I heard my mother's voice, and I just couldn't believe it. She cried and cried. I cried. We kept saying, "Are you all right?"—"Yes." We lied. I could feel my chest tightening; I thought I would faint. She kept asking about the children: Were they going to school? How were they doing? She said she couldn't remember their faces and asked how much they had grown. Neither of us mentioned Mirsad's death; we just kept crying. She kept saying, "Behka, take care of the children," and she told me that my brother Resad, who had been wounded, was fine now.

I trembled long after the conversation. I don't know how I got through it.

We arrived at a refugee center some 120 kilometers from Prague, on November 28, 1992. Internees from the Trnopolje and Manjaca prison camps had arrived at the center ten days before us. They helped us quite a lot and mixed with us; we all got along well.

In January some young men from the center got into a fight with local boys over a girl in a bar. While we were sleeping, a group of Czechs launched an all-out attack on our building. Everyone was evacuated from the first and second floors to the third and fourth floors. We were upset and scared and the local police quickly intervened. Even the police couldn't stop the attack, so reinforcements were sent in from neighboring towns. Nothing like that happened again.

In April 1993, I started to work in a nursery garden, about sixty kilometers from Straz, picking and tying conifer seedlings. I left for work every morning at six. I was the only woman at the center who worked there. Twelve men from the center worked with me on the same job. We would finish at three in the afternoon and then go back to the center. In May, I started a heavy labor job because it paid more—a maximum of one hundred German marks a month. All this time, I had to leave my girls on their own. The older one, Elvana (born in 1982), went to school, and Ermina (born in 1985) attended an all-day kindergarten.

When the internees' families starting arriving from Bosanska Krajina (from Prijedor and Krupa), our problems increased. Once the families were reunited, they suddenly became bothered by the kind of education the women in our group had, by the names of our children, by mixed marriages. Their intolerance toward us kept growing. In July, the internees and five or six women from our group made a petition to force us to leave. Under pressure, we decided we had to go.

The group of "undesirables"—which numbered eight women with children—arrived at our new camp in Doksy exhausted by the constant stress, fights, threats. I hadn't even unpacked my suitcases and recovered from the shock of it all when I heard the terrible news that my husband, Mirsad, had been killed. It was a hot summer day, the afternoon of July 23. That day I learned that my brother-in-law had called me two or three times to tell me about my husband's death, but they wouldn't tell him where I was or give him the phone number. My Mirso died on July 14, 1993 on Mount Igman, during a furious shelling of the mountain. I learned that he had been buried in Pazaric. He was with the army of Bosnia-Herzegovina when he was killed. I told the children of their father's death that same evening, but they wouldn't believe it. Ermina doesn't believe it to this day.

I have no idea how I managed to survive after that; I only know that it is getting harder by the day, that I keep asking myself whether it isn't all some terrible dream. Why did it have to happen? The only thing left is for me to fight for our children, to raise them and see them into adulthood. I don't think about going back, that won't happen for a long time. I'd go back to Bosnia tomorrow if it were the old, prewar Bosnia, but the one they've invented now, this divided Bosnia, I wouldn't even want to visit, nor do I want to live in somebody else's backyard.

The Czech Republic, November 1993

In this story, Bekha talks about her husband's death on Mount Igman, the high ground south of Sarajevo. Bosnian Serb army forces occupied Mount Igman until mid-August 1993. From that strategic point, they could fire shells into Sarajevo. Behka also mentions the internees from the Trnopolje and Manjaca prison camps. According to human rights workers, the Serb leaders and operators of these camps committed grave violations against humanitarian law — including torture and murder of Muslim prisoners. The international war crimes tribunal approved by the UN Security Council in February 1993 is mandated to prosecute the accused on all sides for alleged violations of humanitarian law, crimes against humanity and war crimes.

In mid-December 1993, Behka Granov and her children moved to Germany. They are reportedly doing well.

M., early thirties, Sarajevo
PAUSE

M. and her American friend A. were sitting at M.'s kitchen table, looking at a large collection of photos from M.'s youth, when the phone rang. M. ran into the bedroom to pick up the phone. After fifteen minutes she returned to the table.

M: I really can't believe it. I can't believe it.

A: What?

M: That was my friend E., the one I showed you in the photographs from my high school.

A: (Doesn't remember E., from the dozens of other names M. had recited in going through her photographs) Oh, uh, huh.

M: I hadn't spoken with him in so long!

A: Where was he calling from?

M: California. He's in California now.

A: (Pause) And when did you hear from him last?

M: Oh, I saw him maybe three years ago.

A: (Politely, but not expecting a real answer) How is he?

M: He's OK now. (Pause, and then nonchalantly) He was one of the ones shot in the "marketplace" massacre. They airlifted him to someplace in Europe. They didn't think he would live for a while.

A: How did he get to California?

M: When he got better, he got refugee status there. But he still is taking medical treatments.

A: (Confused) When did you first hear that he was one of the ones in the "marketplace" massacre?

M: Oh, today. (Long pause) Do you want to see his picture again?

New York, N.Y., U.S.A., January 1995

On February 6, 1994, a 120-millimeter mortar fired into a Sarajevo marketplace killed at least 68 people and wounded 197. Responsibility for the shelling is hotly disputed. Serbs claim that Muslims staged the incident to draw publicity, while Muslims claim that Serbs fired the mortar. The first UN investigation was declared faulty; the second UN investigation declared that the shot could have been fired from either side. Today the controversy continues.

CHILDREN'S VOICES

*"I want to be an airplane
and fly my family back
home."*

*"Your younger brother or
sister [can be] afraid of
everything. And if you are
the older one, you cannot
show your fear. You must
help everyone and not
complain."*

*"So all of them lived happily
ever after in heaven."*

L ife as a refugee forces children to grow up quickly. When their mother falls to pieces, they are the ones who must look after their younger siblings. When none of their adult relatives speak English, they are the ones who must translate for the immigration and welfare officials. When they want to continue their studies, they are often the only ones who can arrange the trip; and once they land alone in a foreign country, they are the only ones who can find a place for themselves in their new communities and back home. They must learn how to dream, think, write upside down; they preserve vitality through death, they exorcise the crime, they warn against the evils of the adult world.

A woman refugee in St. Louis read her daughter's poetry and cried. "I never even knew she wrote poetry and only when she published it, she said to me, 'Mother, that was the only way for me to survive.'" Even more than adults, when children write they do it for particular, personal, and often practical reasons: to understand something, to overcome it, to hide it. When children write poetry about war it only means that in this essence of literature some things get straight: that hatred is a big lie, as Dubravka Ugresic claims in her afterword; that history isn't measured by the span of an individual's lifetime; and that politics isn't understandable even when just and explainable. Because only literature can put in words the unbelievable, pardon the unforgivable, and save the sacrificed.

These writings of children and young adults are not necessarily proofs of talent, but of strength: most of them would have preferred to play with their balls in the courtyard than to publish poetry in our book. But their eyes even without looking have seen very precisely what grownups have missed, and if there is something worth saving from this terrible world, the young ones will certainly be the only ones able to do it.

Majana Burazovic, 12 years old, Bosnia-Herzegovina

DON'T CALL ME THAT WAY

If everybody calls me a refugee,
why do you say that to me?

Some people say
it is my true nickname
but don't call me
that way.

I am a child of flesh and blood too
so don't take me
as a torn bag, not you.

I had myself a ball, a doll
blocks I made towers of
but now it is ashes and smoke all.

I am not an orphan, I am not
lost and found on a street,
I am, like you
by a mother born.

I have eyes, nose, mouth, ears
I have good and bad sides in my soul
have you too that all?

I know how to laugh too
and I know how to cry as well
so don't think if you call me
a refugee that I differ from you.
Look at me well
and you will see yourself.

WHY ME?

Sometimes I ask myself: why am I the one
who can only dream to have
peace, freedom, happiness and whose home is
destroyed
even if I didn't want it.

Why am I the one to whom it is normal
to see dead bodies on the street and the one
who in the cellars listens to
the sound of bombs.

Why am I the one who instead of Prince or Madonna
must listen to the sound of bombs and grenades
and the one who on the street
must take care not to become a sniper's target.

Why am I the one who has to queue in the street
for a tin and the one whose bed
is a thin blanket on a cold floor?

Why am I the one who gets always the same answer:
"You are not the only one, a day will come,
when peace will reign
and when people will be together
just as they used to be."

St. Louis, Mo., U.S.A., March 1995

Majana had been secretly writing poetry since the war began. Her mother did not discover Majana's poems until after the family had been in the United States for some time. Majana's mother said that she was surprised and sad when she realized how much her daughter had understood and suffered from the war, and that she learned it only through her daughter's poetry.

Aldina, 12 years old, Tarevci

BECOMING A FOREIGNER

For me everything started when my uncle and father talked about getting us to a safe place. They wanted to go to Zenica but later they decided to bring us to Slovenia. The next morning we started. The truck came and we all got on board. We were with five families on this truck. They brought us to Bosanski Brod where we were accommodated in a school. That place was shelled all day long. We even had to sleep on the desks. We were very scared because we heard explosions all around us. The smaller kids had to be brought into the cellar because they were too scared and crying all the time. In the cellar they couldn't hear the shells.

The next morning we got on a bus to go to another city. Later we got on the train that brought us finally to Slovenia. In Slovenia we could stay with my father's relatives. We ended up being in their house for two and a half months. It was there that we learned that my youngest uncle had been wounded. This uncle was the one who told me that my father and another uncle had died in the war. The news of course hit me very hard. My mother and an aunt who was also in Slovenia decided to move into a refugee home. The apartment in which we were staying was already very full: four families living in a very small space. It was embarrassing for my mother and aunt to be such a burden to the family, so we moved into a former soldiers' barracks.

From this place we went to Koprivnica where we were put in a school and there we stayed a month. It was nice in Koprivnica, we had everything, just in the night Croat soldiers always came and took women who were of legal age (over 18) or those who didn't have kids. They took them away. They took the women with them to the front line to cook for the soldiers. Those women were even brought back to Bosnia. Every time when the guards entered the room in which we slept my mother was afraid they would take her also. My brother and I were underage, but you never know. I just know that all of us had to get up and show our refugee identification cards. Every time when we thought the soldiers were coming, the women hid everywhere. I know one case when a woman was taken away and her daughter cried and begged them not to take her. They just laughed and told her to come also. But she didn't want to go. After three or four days that woman was returned, but there were also many women who never returned.

We learned that we could put our names on a list for a trip to Germany. Because my mother and aunt were afraid to stay in Koprivnica, they put our names on the list. My aunt has a seventeen-year-old daughter so she was especially afraid. I don't know what the soldiers did to the women and girls, but I know it was something very bad.

We got called from the list for Germany so from Koprivnica we went to Varazdin where we got on a train. We were welcomed very warmly in the train. Everything that we needed to eat and drink was waiting for us. It was just great.

We arrived in Osnabruck and were put into soldiers' barracks. It was very nice and we felt good. There we stayed two months. Those who wanted to leave could get themselves transferred into smaller refugee homes or trailers. We got registered to go to Hermannsburg. The people who met us here were very friendly. Each family got their own room and everything they needed. I live here now and I go to school here.

I still hope my father is still alive but we haven't heard anything for two years. My greatest wish would be to know something about him and to know that he is coming to us so we could be all together. Then it wouldn't matter to me if we could go back to Bosnia or not. We could live here as a family quite well, but without him we are all sad. I have many relatives who stayed in Bosnia. One uncle is in Zenica with his family, one aunt is in Samac—they say that she is in a prison camp with her sons. I am here in Hermannsburg but there are many things I cannot forget. I have seen such horrible things and I often dream about them, and I remember the time in Croatia when soldiers beat up men refugees and made them return to Bosnia. The men had to hide everywhere and they cried a lot and everyone was frightened.

The school here is very nice. The teachers are just fine, but there are some bad kids that harass us with words like "foreigners out" and other things like that. I feel very miserable that I have to hear that. Life as a refugee is very hard. In such situations, I feel horrible and all I want is the kids to stop doing these things to us. Sometimes I feel like I'm inferior. Not all the kids do this, there are some nice ones too and when the teachers hear such harassment of course they react. They scold the kids not to do it again or they inform their parents. Sometimes it is very bad because there are some kids who turn directly to us and put their hands up and say things like "heil Hitler." Of course we get frightened though I don't necessarily understand all of it. If we say something against it, they will reply that we are just foreigners and that we have no rights to say anything. We better be quiet. We don't know what they are planning so we don't want to argue with them.

In my class there has never been a discussion on the war in Bosnia-Herzegovina. If there were a discussion, this would perhaps show the kids that we are not here out of our own will. We had in Bosnia a very very nice home, just like the German kids here. But I believe that most of these kids wouldn't be interested in the topic.

They didn't experience something like that and they couldn't feel it. I think if I told some of the kids about the war and what happened to us, some would laugh at me and say, "What does she know?" But maybe some of them would listen. I think our teacher would listen; he also is sad about our fate. This isn't much comfort though because all we want is to be left alone at school and not harassed. With some kids we can't even speak about these things because they had too nice a childhood to think about war. They prefer to talk about hobbies and other nice things.

At class we cannot keep up because our knowledge of German isn't good. Our teachers take extra time with us and help us. We have a woman teacher who is very happy when we volunteer because we think we can answer something. But mostly we keep quiet because we are afraid we will say something wrong and get laughed at. There are even some kids who will help us pronounce things.

I hope many people will read my story and become more understanding.

Hermannsburg, Germany, 1994

This story was told in German and translated and edited by Katrin Kremmler. It made its way to The Suitcase *thanks to Reverend Klaus Burckhardt.*

Teo Brkic, 15 years old, Mostar

THE AMERICAN DREAM

I lived on the Croatian side of the city. The Serbs bombed us, but we had no big problems with them. I left because of the Croats. I lived with my mother on the Croatian side of Mostar while all the rest of my family was on Bosnian territory. That is how I lived until August the 18th of 1993. Then one day the Croats got us, my mother and I; they put us in the concentration camp. But let me tell you the whole story.

I come from the river Neretva, from swimming. I make myself a sandwich and I sit down. Somebody knocks on the door. Come in, why knock? My door was always open. Two Muslim guys I know come in. "Have you packed?" they say. "We heard you want to fight the war. Come on, we are taking you for an exchange." My mother comes home from work at that moment. We pack three plastic bags and they take us straight to the concentration camp. The exchange was only an excuse. There we stayed for four and a half months.

They separated me from my mother, they treated me as a man, not as a child; I was thirteen at that time. Every day I worked thirteen hours: I dug the trenches, I cleaned the houses, whatever they told me. They beat me just for fun, any reason was good: my hairstyle, my earring. We were sixty in one garage of two by four meters. I was the youngest and there were four or five seventy-year-olds. We lived there. The food was good, but there was no medicine. There were Muslim spies among us who told the Croats what we complained about. So they knew whom to beat up.

When the army broke the front line they thought of killing us all. But then one night they came in, they tied our hands and legs with ropes and they took us barefoot across the mountains, on the rocks. They made us sing. We walked like that for hours; the Chetnik snipers shot from the mountains. They made us sing, they humiliated us in every way, and they beat us just for fun. They took us to the heliport, to a big concentration camp. There were something like 15,000 people. It was somehow better there; they didn't beat us. It was only a Muslim camp. They killed the Serbs at once. I spent three months there. An exchange came up, and I passed on the right bank of Mostar. We decided to come to America through the Red Cross. As a prisoner from a camp I could choose the country.

I had always dreamed of America; I made my mother go. It is nice here. I am not going to school anymore; it is closed because the Bosnians had a fight with the Vietnamese. I didn't take part, but I don't want to go to school anymore. Why should I? I am looking for a job. I am already here nine months; I would like to stay another

five or six years, earn some money and if everything settles in Bosnia, go back home and open a pub. That is my dream now.

St. Louis, Mo., U.S.A., April 1995

*As Teo explains, while Serb forces shelled Mostar, much of the fighting took
place between Croats, who controlled one part of the city, and the Muslims,
who controlled the other. UN officials have compared the Croat-run camps
for Muslims around Mostar to the concentration camps in World War II.
Teo's reference to "Chetnik snipers" means Bosnian Serb snipers. Teo spoke
to the editors in the Bosnian Club in St. Louis. Looking every bit the typical
hip American teenager, Teo behaved as if he had buried his past and a bright
future was waiting for him.*

Boy, 11 years old, suburb of Sarajevo

LEARNING TO BE JEWISH

When I dream, I see my Sarajevo. My window sill looking down at
the street and my friend Adem's house. My fish on the shelf next to
mom's piano. My friends and I playing soccer. All of us skiing. In
the winter, we could make smoke when we breathed.

There is a man here who sells things in the market. His face is
the face of a man from my town. He smiles at me when I look at
him. He is a kind man.

I have some new friends here, and I'm learning a new language.
I'm learning what it means to be Jewish. I never knew everything
you had to do! Learning here is a lot of work because everything is
new. But I am a good student.

Sometimes we got to the beach and we play in the sand. Even
though we see soldiers here, they aren't shooting their guns at us and
we can be safe here. My mother is less nervous and she tells us that
everything will be better if we study hard. She has to go to school
too. She studies the language. I can help her with her lessons.

I wish I could run in the street and meet a dozen kids speaking my language. I wouldn't care who they were or where they were from. We wouldn't have to go to the sea or eat anything. Maybe we could just find some empty place and play soccer.

Jerusalem, Israel, January 1995

Sarajevo had a prewar Jewish population of around one thousand residents. In April 1992, despite the heavy Serb shelling of Sarajevo, Jewish organizations evacuated at least 400 Jews from the city, along with a number of non-Jews. Fearful of a resumption of World War II atrocities, many Jews from Sarajevo also left through their own means. Many traveled through Belgrade, where they were helped by the local Jewish population and international humanitarian organizations. According to the Jewish community in Belgrade, their numbers swelled during the war, drawing Jews from all parts of Bosnia. The synagogue in Belgrade installed metal detectors and guards at the doors, as they no longer recognized all members of their community and they feared the increased intolerance in Serbia, which included sporadic anti-Semitic incidents. Some Bosnian Jews stayed in Belgrade; others continued on to Israel and other countries. This story was told to an Israeli peace worker.

Zana, 12 years old, Sarajevo

WHEN FATHER IS IN WAR

If you only knew how it feels
to have Father in war
you run away from unhappiness and unhappiness comes after you
you have no news about your father
and one day when everything becomes black
Father knocks at your door
stays five days
and then happiness goes away again
and my hearts beats strong as a small clock
and now I cannot write anymore because my father
is not here, next to me.

Zehra, Sarajevo

DEAR COUSIN JASMIN

Dear Cousin Jasmin,

Today Mother is baking a cake. She also will make balls of rice. We have discovered many recipes, and when everything will be over, God help us, we will give many of them to you.

You can bake cakes without eggs and butter. You should only see what we manage to do with Eurocream and with the humanitarian aid.

So don't worry about us. I think of you very often.

Your cousin, Zehra

Edina, 12 years old, Sarajevo

RUINS

In my dreams I wander through the ruins
in the old part of the city
looking for a stale piece of bread.
My mother and I inhale the smoke
of the gunpowder
and we imagine it is the smell
of cake and kebab.
We run even if it is nine o'clock in the evening
and maybe we are running toward our grenade,
then an explosion echoes in the street of dignity,
many people are wounded
sisters, brothers, mothers and fathers.
I approach and touch a wounded hand
I touch the death,
terrified I realize it is not a dream,
it is only another day in Sarajevo.

The above three contributions, from Zana, Zehra, and Edina, were originally collected in 1993 by journalist and writer Anna Cataldi, ed., Sarajevo: Voci da un assedio. While these children are not technically "refugees," the editors wanted to include them as the children were living like refugees in their own country.

Ana Despotovska, 10 years old, Croatia

A SAD STORY

One night something was banging. Mother got up, opened the door and somebody killed her. Blood was everywhere around the door. When the daughter woke up, she screamed. So the whole house woke up. Father and brother asked what had happened. She told them. The next day they all went to the grave. When they came back, Father went to mend something, the brother was watching television, and the daughter was alone in the room. Suddenly she heard a voice.

—Who is it? she asked.

—It is I, your mother.

—How come you are here? the daughter asked.

—I came to help you.

—But I don't see you.

—It doesn't matter, don't tell anyone I was here. Father is in the kitchen and I will clean the rooms.

—All right.

—Tomorrow night slip out and come to my grave. And don't be afraid, no one will kill you because I will protect you. But I can't let Father worry. Please come.

—All right.

When the next night came, the girl slipped out of the house. She came to her mother's grave. The image of her mother appeared. The girl asked:

—How come I see you now?

—That's why I called you. I am a ghost during the day and a woman at night. That is, I live in the sky.

—Is it nice there?

—Without you, your father and your brother, it isn't.

—How can we get there?

—By mourning me.

When she came home the whole family began to cry and every night they went to heaven. One day the daughter fell ill and died. The father and brother were so sad that they too died quickly. So all them lived happily ever after in heaven.

Belgrade, Serbia, May 1994

Ana wrote this story for a creative writing class that Jasmina Tesanovic held in a Belgrade school. "This was not the assigned topic," Jasmina remembers, "but it was the only story the girl could tell." Ana is now with her family in Canada.

Mujo Mustafic, 11 years old, Bosnia-Herzegovina
YOU WON'T FIND ME HERE

I am not here and I don't exist.
In my city sunshine and blossoms
and some stranger's hand is stealing
the scent of the summer and silk of the treasury.

I am not here, but my soul
struggles all evening on every tiny street
and a lily clings on to a lapel
and plants a tree next to every home.

Almina Kotoric, 11 years old, Bosnia-Herzegovina

IF I WERE AN APPLE

If I were an apple, I would like to be eaten by the hungry children of Bosnia. I wouldn't like to wither like a flower or rot on a branch. But, apples don't go to school and they don't play. Just like people, apples are not the same. If I were an apple, thrown away in basket, I might be eaten even by a war. Altogether I wouldn't like to be an apple, because my sister would eat me.

The above two poems, by Mujo and Almina, were written as part of a children's writing workshop held by refugee organizations in Slovenia, and they were originally published in the refugee magazine Izi: Refugees for Refugees.

Ksenija, 8 years old, Belgrade

GOD WAS HEARD ON EARTH

There was a man called Branko. While he was at home the telephone rang. Branko answered and heard: he had to go to war. So he got a rifle and uniform and he went. When he came, war broke out. While he was shouting he heard a voice which led him closer and closer to the enemy. He wondered who could it be? And when he came to the enemy, they killed him and he went to Paradise. When he came there he saw who led him to the enemy: it was God. He dragged me to Paradise so he wouldn't be alone.

Vienna, Austria, June 1992

Ksenija wrote this story while she was in exile in Vienna because people in Belgrade were afraid that Belgrade would be bombed. She doesn't like writing or reading. She said that she wrote this story using the computer of her very grown-up Austrian friend because she didn't have children to play with, and because she wanted to tell her Austrian friends that not all Serbs are bad.

Ksenija returned to Belgrade with her mother, who works on various actions for peace and multiculturalism.

Ivan, 11 years old, Konjic

WHAT HAPPENED TO YOU?

When it all began, I mean the war, we left. We left by car. It was at night, about one o'clock in the morning. They told us we all had to go out of the house and leave the town. We got on buses and then we arrived at a water pump and then we set out for Belgrade. I know where some of my friends are now: Blanka and Miljana went to Sweden, Damir—a boy we called Ilic—he went to Finland. The others, I forgot their names, went to Montenegro.

I would like to go back home. I used to play soccer with my friends Srdjan, Aldin, Damir and Moamer. We lived close, in one or two blocks of flats. Moamer was killed, a grenade hit him. Also, my friend Aldin was hit by a bullet when he was sleeping. I don't know what to say about that. . . .

I miss many things, like there I had a video recorder, and we had some cartoons. I used to switch them on and watch them and other programs. My favorite serial was about a funny family. I remember my bicycle. We left it in the cellar.

I am here now and I like the place, but still I miss my daddy. He is still there. . . . Once he was wounded and when he recovered he phoned us. I know how to use guns: a rifle has a butt, and there is a trigger. You hold the trigger. Then you press the trigger and you fire. You can change it from the side.

Here, I watch TV, go to school. Sometimes they don't understand at school. I speak like we used to speak in Konjic. Everything is so different. I hope to go back, even though Mummy says we probably will never ever go back there.

Belgrade, Serbia, 1994

Konjic has an unfortunate position in the political geography of Herzego-vina. It was the site of intense Croat-Muslim fighting and, at the same time, it lies very near Serb-controlled territory. In April 1993, the Washington Post *described Croat-Muslim fighting in Konjic as dwarfing all earlier strife between the two groups. Ivan and his family left in April 1993. He gave this interview to a French journalist and a member of the Belgrade peace group* Women in Black.

Admir, 13 years old, Gorazde

WAITING FOR HOME

I came to the hospital in Zemun (Belgrade) on the tenth of March, 1992, for an operation [unrelated to the war]. I lay there until the tenth of April and then I was sent to the Institute for Mothers and Children. I stayed there until the sixth of August and then I came here to live in the collective center for refugees in Kovilovo. The war started when I was having my operation. I was supposed to go home and go to Sarajevo for radiation treatment.

The doctor told me I could go after I had radiation treatment and lay every day in the hospital. . . . When we were waiting for me to finish and go home, the war started and the doctor told me that I would stay in the hospital with them.

Mummy and Daddy are in Srebrenica, Bosnia, with my brothers and sisters. All of my family is there. I am here alone. I have heard from them and Daddy that they are well and healthy. I told them that I am well too and that I have no problems here. My Daddy calls me through the ham radio. I ask him when I can go home. He tells me that I should wait a little longer and then we'll see.

I miss them all. I haven't seen anybody since the third of April, 1992. I wish to hug them so much. I don't know how to express it. I dream a lot. A few nights ago, I dreamt that my uncle and

Daddy were building a house. They were making something. I was with them and I was shouting to Daddy that I didn't want to go to school.

Zemun, Serbia, 1994

Less than two weeks after Admir left home for his cancer treatment, fighting broke out between Serbs and Bosnian Muslims and Croats in Gorazde. Serb forces kept Gorazde under siege for months at a time, sporadically cutting all access to food and supplies. U.S. planes airdropped supplies into Gorazde (and other cities) in Bosnia-Herzegovina. Although Gorazde was eventually declared a safe area by the UN Security Council (on May 6, 1993), peace never came for long. Admir, a young boy from a Muslim community, was stuck in the heart of Serbia. He told his story to a volunteer for Women in Black. As of this writing, he is still separated from his parents.

Jelena, 9 years old, Sarajevo

UNTITLED

I lived in Sarajevo. Our house was a big one. The upper story was in red brick and the lower in stone. My mother used to work as a medical doctor. She wore a nice dress and walked around the hospital.

I am here with Nikola, Nemanja and Mummy and that's all. My daddy was killed there. I don't know how. Grandpa came and told us that Daddy was in prison. He told us to leave. We went by bus at about five o'clock. Then the shooting started again. I don't know how it happened, but they told me that I don't have a father anymore. My mummy cried, together with our neighbor Milena and my brothers.

In the beginning, I dreamt that I was playing with him. Last night, I dreamt that I was on a sleigh and that an old woman was hugging me around the neck and that I pushed her over the balcony.

She was the sort of old person who wears strange dresses. I looked for a hole in the dress but there wasn't one. There wasn't even a dress or a head. She didn't have any teeth.

Belgrade, Serbia, 1994

Jelena lives with her family in a refugee camp near Belgrade. She was interviewed by a refugee worker for the International Red Cross.

Mirsada Salihovic, 9 years old, Bosnia-Herzegovina
I WISH I HAD A MASK

If I could have a mask, I would want it to be authentic.
I would like my mask to be in the shape of the sun.
Then I would, in the cold winter days, put my mask on
my face and I would warm my sister and all the children
who are cold.

If I had a mask of sunshine, I would then be above
Bosnia where I would heat my people and all
the children and my father, and even more.
If my wish were to come true, that I was truly the sun,
my mask would allow me to see my father!

Mirsada wrote this as part of a children's writing workshop for Izi: Refugees
for Refugees; *it originally appeared in the* Izi *magazine.*

Erna Susic, 17 years old, Mostar
THE TELEPHONE NUMBER

It's scary. It's scary when I think about genocide and victims in my country.
Sometimes, I cannot understand people's feelings when they lose

somebody in the family. But I can understand children's feelings who are separated from their families, mother and father, because I am one of these children. I was separated from my family when I was fifteen years old. Now, I am almost eighteen. Between fifteen and eighteen was the period when I needed my parents most. I had to work at sixteen and worry about my bread for tomorrow. It was hard and it still is, because I am still without my parents.

My parents stayed in Mostar, Bosnia-Herzegovina. For one year I didn't hear their voices or get their letters. I've just found a telephone number to call them after all this time.

I was very happy when my friend gave me the number. But at the same time I was nervous and the first thoughts that came to my mind were what to say to my parents after one year without letters or words. But I didn't want to think about that. I just wanted to call, to hear their voices, to be sure that they are still alive.

But the telephone number is not even the telephone number of my parents. I can call them only indirectly.

I called one day and spoke to a man. He told me that he will try to find my parents and asked me to call him in few days. These days are coming and I have to call again. But I am still nervous, happy and nervous and I am thinking what to say to them. I will say that I love them very much.

New York, N.Y., U.S.A., June 1994

Erna is now attending college in the United States and is doing very well. She hasn't seen her parents since she left home, but she can talk to them more frequently. She plans to go back home eventually to help build her country.

Alisa Mujagic, 20 years old, Kozarac

A STUDENT'S STORY

In August 1992, I left my country of Bosnia and Herzegovina for Croatia. I thought that would be the end of the hell, the beginning of life, of human happiness, where my pain could be forgotten just as one forgets a nightmare. But in Croatia what I felt was only another form of ethnic cleansing and discrimination. I felt trapped. I wanted to run away from the evil that was following and torturing me, but I realized my escape would only please my executioner.

So I stayed. I first worked for a year as a volunteer in a refugee camp in Croatia. Most of the children seven years and older were denied access to school. As a Muslim, I, too, was refused all education. Before the war in Croatia, two thousand Bosnian students were attending college. In 1992 the Croatian government abolished all Muslim students' rights while the Croatian students were still allowed to go to school.

My friends and I understood that education was essential to our future, to the future of our country. We organized the Association of Students from Bosnia and Herzegovina. Our purpose was to protect and preserve the rights of Bosnian students. Serbs, Croats, and Muslims were members. In our association everyone who felt a responsibility to future generations was welcome.

Through one of our association's projects, I was able to come to the United States to finish my last year of high school. Getting an exit visa as a refugee from a town occupied by Serbs was not easy. But with the help of an American in Mostar, I made it to New Hampshire by November 1993.

Today I live in Exeter, New Hampshire, where I go to school. I guess I should be happy. I can eat whatever I want. I don't have to be afraid anymore. But my soul is empty and cold. What is left is a 40-year-old woman in a 20-year-old body. I cannot even see the graves of my friends, the grave of my native town.

Finishing high school was just one step toward my goal. Next I must go to college so I can go back and build my Bosnia. I have applied for financial aid at some colleges and I hope that I will be able to go. I am quickly learning that little people are the generous ones, not big institutions. In the end I don't need charity, I need what belongs to me, what was taken from me—my education. I need an education now more than ever as the only way to get back my future, my country's future.

Sometimes I phone my mom. She is hoping that we can be together again in Kozarac, my native town. As spring approaches, I want my Bosnia so much. I feel her warm soul, I smell the scent of blossoms. I am anxious to see my friends. I want to go *home*. Here is not my place. Here I see how people enjoy life, with no knowledge of Bosnia. My country is waiting for me, the same Bosnia I left in her fragrant, white dress of blossoms. My happiness is there, with my family and my friends.

"What did it matter if we existed for two or twenty years? Happiness was the fact that we existed," said Albert Camus. I want more than to exist. I want to be happy. I want my friends and family back. I want my homeland back. I want to belong.

Exeter, N.H., U.S.A., 1994

Alisa is now attending college in the United States and hopes to return home. Her home town, Kozarac, near Prijedor, is now Serb-controlled.

Sandra Alisic, 15 years old, Mostar

EMIR AND I

Bosnia. It is Saturday. My best friend Emir is coming here, to my house. We will play chess, as on every Saturday. Fun! What can be more relaxing?

There is silence. We move the pieces slowly. We think. A few sounds from outside intrude on our peace. The hours pass. The game is finished.

Now there is music. We play the accordion and the piano. And talk. We eat cookies. This is our Saturday. Next week, I'll go to Emir's house.

New York. Two years later, Saturday. I am here. Emir is here, too. We continue our tradition of playing chess, after many months apart. There is the same silence, the pieces move just as slowly.

But the peace is not the same, the house and the country are different, too. Now it is not just about having fun, and relaxing. It is something more. It is a connection to the past, a fleeting moment when I can reclaim something of my old life.

Maybe next week, there will be music.

New York, N.Y., U.S.A., May 1994

Sandra is a student in the United States.

Tomaz Jurancic, early teens, Bosnia-Herzegovina

NO TITLE

Nightfall. A dark, never-ending evening. And snow. Wind. A strong, cold wind. A handful of people defeat the battle of the night, snow and wind, everything is getting smaller. Many have already succumbed to the night, many more will before they find an adequate place to start a foundation for civilization . . .

Struggle. People thrusting each other like black shadows. Arms and shells irradiate. Just over there somebody climbs onto a horse, like the wind he breezes across the field, lifts the cutting edge scant above the enemies' head, in full swing . . .

The leader of the country leans over the letter. He has to write just one word which can push many people toward death. He lifts his pen and writes "WAR" . . .

Nightfall. A dark, a never-ending evening. And snow. Wind. A strong, cold wind. A handful of people who . . .

Time passes, similarly it repeats itself whenever people constantly make the same mistake. Perhaps another face, but undoubtedly the same errors. First they fight to survive, then they establish themselves and in the end destruction sets in.

Time passes, but still the only witness to those happenings are the never-ending recurrences. Why exactly am I living to write this composition?

All the same, everything, that is everything, repeats itself.

Tomaz wrote this as a school composition; it was published by Izi: Refugees for Refugees *in Ljubljana, Slovenia.*

Girl, late teens, Foca
NO ONE TO WORRY

If I could tell the world anything about being a refugee? I can't say just one thing. Being a refugee is like a bad dream that won't go away. Being a refugee means being forgotten, unwanted. Being a refugee means being in a barracks with thin blankets and rotting food with no refrigerator. It means missing school, forgetting everything you once knew, and maybe walking past people who hate you to a school where no one talks your language. It means having old clothes, old blankets, things no one wants because no one wants you. No books. No TV. No laughter.

No one to worry: "Why don't you eat? You look so pale. You're too thin." All of the people who would have said those things before are gone, or they have become something else. I used to hate it when my mother told me to dress warmly, but now I miss it.

If I could tell young people about being a refugee, I would say that it means watching your family fall apart. Your father killed or in war. Your mother so tired and worried all the time. Your younger brother or sister afraid of everything. And if you are the older one, you cannot show your fear. You must help everyone and not complain.

Turkey, 1995

This girl traveled south with her family out of Bosnia-Herzegovina, through Serbia to Macedonia, and then onward to Turkey. She told her story to a refugee worker.

Dunja Metikos, 15 years old, Sarajevo

NUMB

Our lives have to continue.
That is the rule by which I live.
That is my reality and my future.
No matter how hard the living
is, no matter if you are half
alive or not, you have to go
on. Even if they make you so
nervous, even if the anguish
kills you, you have to survive.
You have to fight. Always.

You must realize that you
are alone, or else you will
fail. Do not ever ask anything,
just keep smiling.
Lie, if it is necessary,
but never let them know.

TO MY MOTHER, THANK YOU

Thank you, for you saved me from influence from the inside,
giving me life for a second time.
You brightened my soul.
Thank you, for you told me the story about the world,
you gave me courage to survive.
Thank you, for you healed me from the illness,
I never thought I could believe.
Thank you, for you let me be part of you,
for experience that shall never be forgotten.
You opened up your heart to me,
though I am just a mortal.
Thank you, for you showed me the difference between
wrong and right,
for you are the only one I believe in—
you saved me from death.

THROUGH THE FOG

In the dusk of the well-known room, they talked persistently. They
understand that she went through so many terrible things. They
realize that it is not easy—not at all. They all know how she feels.
But they know she is brave. They know she will make it. They
know her.

She kept silent. She did not hear them. She hid her hands in the
pockets and squeezed them. While she was nodding her head, she
ground her teeth.

Through her half-opened eyes, she watched the expression on
their faces. All those faces uncovering the truth.

She was sitting deaf and mute in the closed room. She was tired
of being sad. She looked at the book [lying] beside her with fatigue.
The only real object in the room. She took the book and squeezed
it so hard that her hands started hurting. The tear rolled down her

face. Suddenly she felt a strange vibration through her body and a rapid twitch. She threw the book down.

She looked at them, picked up the book and foolishly smiled.

Lisbon, N.D., U.S.A., 1994–1995

Dunja wrote the preceding two poems and this story while she was separated from her mother, Habiba, and living with an American family in Lisbon, North Dakota. Habiba had sent her to the United States from Zagreb (where they both were refugees from Sarajevo — see the story "Conversion" by Habiba Metikos in the section "Starting Life Anew," below). That was the fourth time Dunja had moved in three years. She had gone with her mother first to Germany, then she went alone to Canada, then she had joined her mother in Zagreb — and now America.

Dunja moved again one year later — to Canada. Habiba had received an immigration visa to Canada and Dunja moved to be with her; Dunja's father is still in Sarajevo. These were the last contributions gathered for The Suitcase. *Habiba, one of the preparers of* The Suitcase, *did not know about her daughter's writing until sharing with Dunja a draft of the book. Dunja cried at the other stories and then brought out her own contribution — an illustrated notebook binder filled with neatly penned entries. All her pieces, including these selections, were written in English.*

The suitcase. Photo by
Branko Pantelic.

The police came and said, "You must go, you must be packed and ready to go." Photo by Dragan Milovanovic.

All the trailer could hold. Photo by Dragan Milovanovic.

*Sarajevo — what was
"the most beautiful city in
the world" is now a
shooting range. Photo by
Zeljko Jovanovic.*

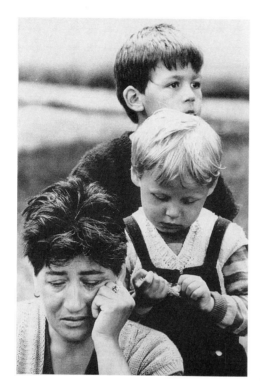

From day to day. Photo by Vladimir Dimitrijevic.

Refugees from Foca, Bosnia, who ended up in Kosovo: "I have bad dreams too." Photo by Julie Mertus.

Waiting — when there is
nothing else to be done.
Photo by Pedja Mamuzic.

*Model town built by Bos-
nian refugees in Pakistan:
"So we would not forget."
Photo by Muriz Cemer.*

*Authors of group poems
in Pakistan. Photo by
Julie Mertus.*

"They call him their puppet father." Mother makes a puppet father so the children won't miss their real one so much. Vienna, Austria. Photo by Radmila Bartel.

*Boredom and no
privacy — growing up
in a collective refugee
center. Photo by
Pedja Mamuzic.*

Mira's daughter stands before the abandoned schoolhouse they use for a home. Photo © Lisa Kahane, 1994.

*Waiting to leave
Srebrenica. Photo by
Zeljko Safer.*

Trying to be good.
Photo by Rade Prelic.

First night under a roof
for refugees from Krajina.
Photo © Lisa Kahane,
1995.

*Dreams of home in a
gymnasium of strangers,
Serbia. Photo © Lisa
Kahane, 1995.*

*Lunchtime at Rosa
House — a woman-run
shelter in Zagreb, Croatia.
Photo by Center for
Women War Victims.*

*Among the last to leave
Vukovar. Photo by
Vladimir Dimitrijevic.*

A final glance, Vukovar,
Croatia. Photo by
Vladimir Dimitrijevic.

Resident of Rosa House.
Photo by Vesna Kesic.

Crossing the border —
a very old woman with
a young woman soldier.
Photo by Zoran Mrdja.

*"I want a normal life, not a
refugee life — I want to not
depend on anyone, to live
off of my own work, to
help my relatives in Bosnia
with my own work."*

*"I'm trying to learn the
language as quickly as
possible. I don't want
anyone to recognize my
accent. I'm sick of
answering questions."*

*"There is nothing left for me
in this life. But I try
because of my children.
Maybe they can have a
little happiness."*

Life in forced exile has little in common with voluntary emigration: the refugee had no wish for a new life, was not hoping to upgrade or remake the old one. There is no certain path to follow. Only through concentrated effort can one in forced exile keep remembering to forget, to begin again. When buses pull into town with new arrivals, when the television set blares scenes from war into living rooms, when a letter or phone call from a friend comes unexpectedly, refugees recoil, and perhaps lapse for a moment or a day or a month into thinking that they themselves have just arrived, that they themselves are again in the war zone. Then, quietly, the survivors begin again. And those refugees who find the strength to reconstruct the path of their life may be crazy enough to consider themselves lucky.

Some refugees stumble upon a person or an organization that helps, a woman's group, a humanitarian group, friends or strangers who support the slow process of believing again in life and in oneself. They pass language exams after studying on the bus to and from work, they wash dishes in restaurants until their backs sag, they buy meat every night for dinner (which they could never afford before), they help newer arrivals who have even less than they do. Well practiced at being resilient, the exiled improvise when all else fails. When her daughters miss their father so much they will not sleep, one woman makes a "puppet father"—a puppet looking just like their father that the girls can play with all day long. When Americans greet her with seemingly silly, superficial friendliness, a Bosnian makes notes about each curious Americanism to share with friends. When the first paycheck comes, many refugees find some creative way to send a bit to their relatives back home. And not all refugees are innocents; some may even push other civilians out of their homes in order to create space for themselves.

Some refugees accept their newfound identities with irony and humor: they change their national identities (Bosnians become Jews), or their professional lives (doctors become assembly-line workers), or their psychological state (the deadened become alive). Some take the life of exile as a serious vow of rebirth: "Please do not write us. . . . We do not want to be reminded of anything." In any case, refugees who want to become integrated into a new land must juggle absolute forgetting with those obstinate memories of culture, language, and family that stubbornly hang on. Refugees sacrifice pride—if not for themselves, many parents say, then for the sake of the children, who will speak in a new language of a new people. Refugee parents may burn their identities to light a new fire, in a new land. In thirty years, perhaps, the grass of indifference will cover the path of arrival, hiding the traces of who wished to come and who was forced. But the price refugees had to pay can never be compared with that of the willing emigrant. Try though they may, refugees can never forget.

Anonymous family, Bosnia-Herzegovina
DON'T REMIND US

We arrived here safely. Everyone is fine. Please do not write us or try to contact us. We do not want to be reminded of anything.

Canada, 1994

This is from a postcard sent by one refugee family to another refugee family still in Pakistan.

Woman, 30s, Sarajevo

CANDLES

My grandmother lit candles. And she never left Sarajevo. She told us stories about the wars, about hiding in cellars, about the shells that fell in the cemetery. It was like a romantic movie for us. A foreign country. We would never be in cellars. We would never have bombs. And although we still had candles, the Jewish part of ourselves would never again be connected with hiding, with fleeing. We were Sarajevans, Bosnians, Yugoslavs. Of course, we were also Jewish, but I would never answer "Jewish" if someone asked me my nation.

In Israel, of course, I am Jewish first. A Jewish refugee. For this, we can be citizens. We, Jewish refugees, are all here to be safe from people who hate us because we are not like them. This is supposed to be the tie that binds us all together. But really I have little in common with the other Jews here. I am a part of Sarajevo, not Israel. Sometimes I feel guilty about not being Jewish enough here— that I just snuck in and eventually they will find out that I do not deserve to be here.

My daughter is speaking better Hebrew already than I do. She started in school the first month we got here. She instructs me in how to be a better Jew. She is very insistent that I try to learn religious traditions better. I'm sure she learns all that in school. My husband doesn't listen to her or anyone else. He doesn't want to be a good Jew. I try for the sake of my daughter, but I will never be like the mothers of my daughter's friends.

When the war began, we were sure that they would come for the Jews like they always do. We never really went to synagogue before, but we started to go and to listen to the things everyone was saying. When they offered us a place to go to, Israel, my mother said that we should go. We were some of the first ones out. Maybe our Jewish selves saved us this time.

I used to read the paper or listen to the news every day. Now sometimes I skip days. It is too painful. I feel guilty about being here when so many of my friends are back home in Sarajevo. I have nightmares about war. If there was a chance of a war here, I would leave immediately and go anywhere. If I can't be in Sarajevo, at least I want to be in peace.

Jerusalem, Israel, 1995

This story came to The Suitcase *from Israeli peace workers through e-mail.*

Adisa, 27 years old, Tuzla

POSTCARD FOR MEHRUM

When we got here, my son Mehrum was a baby. Seven days ago we celebrated his third birthday. I bought him a blue jumper and a toy truck. I tried hard to be happy. My friends here came with a cake and some ice cream. I cried when I saw them. I watched Mehrum eat his cake and I began to cry again. Mehrum notices when I cry and it upsets him. I try not to let him see me, to cry only when he is asleep, but on his birthday, the day that was to be the happiest day of the year, I couldn't stop crying.

Mehrum was only a baby when we left. He'll never know anything about his fatherland. Now all he knows is this foreign country. He knows only his park, his streets, his room, his toys. This is his world. When someone asks Mehrum where he is from, he knows to answer "I am from Tuzla." But he doesn't know what this Tuzla means. I want to tell him stories about Tuzla, to tell him about his father, his grandparents, but I don't know what to say. I want to wait until he is older and until I can speak without crying. I want him to learn about a Bosnia of laughter and happiness.

We left quickly. My neighbor pushed me onto the convoy. I didn't want to leave. My husband was with his family in the village and I wanted to wait for him, but my neighbor yelled at me, "Think of your child." I always thought he [her husband] would follow us. I even imagined that we would soon return. But now he is dead and I am afraid that I will never return again.

One of the other women from Tuzla here managed to bring some postcards of our city. I wonder how she got such a good idea. She gave me one for Mehrum. I'll save it for another birthday.

Germany, 1995

Despite the May 1993 decision of the UN Security Council making Tuzla a safe area to be patrolled by UNPROFOR, the city continued to be shelled repeatedly by Serb forces. The last major shelling occurred in the spring of 1995, when a group of young people were killed by a shell falling into a Tuzla cafe.

In December 1995, Bosnian President Alija Izetbegovic, Croatian President Franjo Tudjman, and Serbian President Slobodan Milosevic signed a peace treaty in Paris, agreeing to carve Bosnia roughly in half: into a Serb republic and a Muslim-Croat federation, with a weak and seemingly symbolic central government. Under the agreement, both parts of the new entity are allowed close ties with their neighboring countries — the Muslim-Croat federation with Croatia and the Serb republic with "reduced Yugoslavia" (Serbia and Montenegro). The agreement, which had been hammered out the month before in Dayton, Ohio, by Assistant Secretary of State Richard Holbrooke, called for a NATO force of 60,000 to enforce the peace. The United States' share of the force, 20,000 troops, is headquartered in Tuzla, drawing international focus (and American dollars) into the city. As this book goes to press, many refugees have still been unable to return home.

Girl, 13 years old, suburb of Sarajevo
SNIPPETS OF LETTERS HOME

FIRST MONTH IN UNITED STATES

I'm very sorry if you went to the airport to wait for us, but we missed our plane in Athens and had to wait two days for the next. I wish I could have called you from Athens but I didn't have any money. We arrived the next night in Chicago. We are staying in an apartment. It is furnished with secondhand furniture and the neighborhood is a little scary but it's fine.

We still don't have a social security card and we aren't getting "public aid" this month, so our relatives are sponsoring us. Also, I haven't started school yet. But I like it very much and I'm excited.

THIRD MONTH IN UNITED STATES

I started school and already I have my first A. We decided that I should be in a younger class because I missed so much school, but this school is very easy and I don't like it very much. I am in the "talented and gifted" class. My school is in the center of the city and my mother is worried all the time. There is no place to go after school except home.

My parents have to attend English classes at night and I watch my little brother. They are very sad about learning English. I try to help them but they get frustrated. I hope they learn fast because I have too many things to do. I have to translate for them all the time. I talk to all of the public aid people, the aid worker who comes by here sometimes. I worry that they may never learn English.

My brother is still scared. He cries a lot when he sleeps. He hasn't learned English because he doesn't have any American friends here, but as soon as my parents get a job, he'll go to the nursery and I'm sure he'll learn fast.

FIFTH MONTH IN UNITED STATES

We're having summer vacation now so I'm not in school. I spend all the time at home taking care of my brother. This apartment is hot and small, and we have no park outside. I miss the trees of home.

My parents still don't speak English. They are looking for jobs, but they can't find any because they need English. Someone told them they can earn money by cleaning houses and offices, but they are professionals. I think that they should have good jobs.

I have a long list of books for the summer. I am reading all the books I can. I want to improve myself. This country is nothing like I thought it would be. We all wish we were back in Bosnia.

Chicago, Ill., U.S.A., April–July, 1995

The girl in this story taught herself English while in a refugee camp. Although her parents have learned some English themselves, she is still the main person in her family in charge of all communications in English, from paying bills to dealing with social workers. She has received nothing but A's at her public junior high school in Chicago, and she hopes to find a scholarship to a private high school where she will be more challenged. Her parents worry about child kidnapping in the United States and guns in the schools. They forbid their children from walking any more than necessary around their neighborhood, and so their daughter spends most of her time alone reading library books and writing letters (these are excerpts from selected letters). Neither parent has found a job — they live mainly on contributions from other people from ex-Yugoslavia. Although Croats kicked them out of Croatia, their main support comes from Croatian families in the United States.

The family celebrated the signing of the peace agreement in Paris, but still they are skeptical of long-lasting peace. They plan to go back to Bosnia.

F. B., 29 years old, Bosnia-Herzegovina

HAVE A NICE DAY

The man at the envelope factory couldn't believe that I wanted the job. "But you're a doctor," he said. "But my family must eat," I replied. He told me that I would stand next to an assembly line and help guide the envelopes into their boxes. He told me that I would work eight hours a day with a short break in the middle for lunch and that I would have no vacation until I was there for six months. "OK," I said, "When can I start?"

I need enough money to buy a car. No one here in America can get anywhere without a car. So my husband (who is a professor) cleans offices and I work on the assembly line and we both keep looking for extra jobs. Fortunately, we have had day care for our kid since we got here. But I have to pay one hundred dollars a week for day care and that is a big part of my salary. I don't think I can find a better job until I learn English and buy a car. I am so embarrassed whenever I try to say anything. We have classes nearly every night of the week, but we can't afford a babysitter so we take turns attending. We're not very good students.

We have been eating meat every day since we got here. We hadn't eaten it regularly in so long! And it is so cheap here compared with Bosnia and Croatia. I am getting sick of meat, but I can't stop buying it.

Americans are very friendly. Even people who don't know us at all say "Hello" and the people in stores are always saying "Have a nice day" and "How can I help you" and other nice things. But all these words are very thin. We have made few friends here. No one invites you to their house or out for a coffee. And no one seems to care much after "Have a nice day." I am afraid sometimes to talk to people because I fear that once they discover I'm a refugee, they'll just feel pity for me.

I am glad that we landed here in America because at least we are not alone. There are a lot of Bosnians here and we can see each other, laugh, cry, sing. But I rarely have time. Being in America means working all the time.

Whenever I can, I send money home to my mother and father. I find some way to get them something. One thing I've learned from being a refugee is that anything is possible. In Bosnia, I saw the dark side of those possibilities; I am now trying to see some light.

St. Louis, Mo., U.S.A., July 1995

As of the signing of the peace agreement in December 1995, F. B.'s home town still remained in Bosnian Serb hands. F. B., who comes from a Muslim community, hopes to return to home regardless — at least to somewhere in Bosnia. She is waiting to see what happens.

Katica, mid 30s, Banja Luka

BITS AND PIECES

I am behaving strangely, I don't recognize myself. I am lost, I am scared, I don't communicate. That is not me. That is the refugee, as they call me. Without a home, without work, without any conditions for a normal life. Everything is destroyed; only some bits and pieces have remained, which depend on somebody's hand: these may be destroyed in the end, thrown away invisible, or put together with a loving hand in some loving place. I still meet hands who want to adjust things, to construct things, even these bits and pieces, finding their original value in them. . . .

Renewed by somebody else's hands, I am able to renew other bits and pieces, which unfortunately are more numerous every day and which need my hands to be loved, taken care of, and hopefully renewed.

Zagreb, Croatia, March 1995

This is part of a much longer story Katica wrote in a workshop given by the Center for Women War Victims in Zagreb, an autonomous women's group that has been working with women refugees of all ethnonational identities since the war began. Her home town, Banja Luka, became a Bosnian Serb stronghold in the beginning of the war, and as of the signing of the December 1995 peace accords, it remains in Bosnian Serb hands. Katica does not want to return to a divided Bosnia, nor does she want to stay in Croatia.

M., 43-year-old woman, Odzak

SOCIAL AID

I am used to working and to living on my own earnings. All of my life I worked in a firm in Odzak, and my husband and I had built a nice house. Before the war, many Serbs and Croats visited us and everyone got along well, but the war has destroyed everything. Now here in Hermannsburg I've become a totally different person. I miss my freedom and my home very much. It is especially difficult to have to rely on social aid. At home I didn't even know what that was. Now when I have to go to get my social aid I feel very miserable. First I get a big big lump in my throat and I blush and I am so ashamed. Still, I'm grateful for the help and people are always very nice to us and I appreciate everything they give us.

Of course I know that no one can give me back my freedom and my home, but I always live with the hope that I may return home. I would never put up with spending my life anywhere else but in Odzak. Should I ever return to Bosnia, then only to Odzak. Every other city would be foreign to me. I would as well stay in Hermannsburg. Only my Odzak is my home.

Hermannsburg, Germany, 1995

Odzak is in northeastern Bosnia-Herzegovina, near the border with Croatia. Bosnian Serb forces took control of this entire region in October 1992, thus connecting Serb lands, providing a land channel from the self-proclaimed

Serbian Republic of Krajina to Serbia. One issue that could not be decided during the November 1995 Dayton peace talks was the matter of the "Brcko corridor," the thinnest part of Serb-controlled land connecting Serb-held territories. According to the Dayton agreement, arbitration will decide control over Brcko. Because this region, located east of Odzak, may be a particularly tender spot for some time to come, M. will not likely return home soon.

Woman, 35 years old, Sarajevo

THOSE WHO HAVE NOTHING HELP

I went out of Sarajevo in 1994 to my relatives in Vojvodina. I worked in an import/export business before the war, but I was fired because I was Orthodox. My husband stayed to work. As you see, we are in a mixed marriage. His pay was half a mark per month. Our relatives, refugees in Serbia and Croatia, sent us money to survive.

When I went out with my six-year-old daughter we moved from one relative to another. They would provoke me because my husband stayed in Sarajevo even though he didn't fight in the army. It is chaos in Vojvodina; they know nothing about what is going on. They all want to fight the war but if something really would explode in there, they would run away to Romania.

We were without papers. Without money. My well-situated family hardly helped me. They made me do all kinds of humiliating jobs to pay for the food we were eating. At the end I moved in with some other refugees who had nothing like me and we shared everything.

We were among the last ones to get out. We stayed to the very end hoping that it would stop. All of our friends had already left for Canada, Munich, Chicago, Vienna, New Zealand. When we decided to go, friends from all nationalities helped us; otherwise we couldn't have made it, because you need special permits from all three sides. We were staying in a house of Muslims in Sarajevo and they told us: "Nothing will happen to you while we are alive. We will all die together if we must." We have an obvious surname [Serbian]; I didn't dare move out of the house because of it, but my husband ignored it.

My daughter passed the war completely unconscious. Thank God she is young. Even playing in the cellar during bombings can be fun. But still she is nervous while asleep, sometimes she cries without any reason, and she is afraid of every loud sound. And she cannot sleep alone.

We are waiting for our paper to go to Canada and we will take our parents with us. We already have many friends there. When we are together again, it still won't be as it used to be. We will be nostalgic about our past lives, we will cry over our old songs. I still cannot understand how it all happened.

Camp Bicke, 30 km from Budapest, Hungary, May 1995

This woman, who wishes to remain anonymous, told her story while sitting on a park bench in front of her barrackslike dwelling. Her daughter played with a friend on a blanket on the dirt ground, and her husband paced about impatiently, waiting to go to the collective center for lunch. The family left for Canada shortly after giving this interview. They do not want to return to Bosnia.

Eleonora Birsl, 23 years old, Sarajevo
UNTITLED

What is left behind me?
Nineteen years of wonderful living,
my mother in tears,
my big white house,
unforgettable friendships.

Sarajevo,
sleepy in the mist,
startled.
My statistic textbook opened midway,
the essay on morals half accomplished,
one love story, half begun . . .
Half of me left, half of me stayed.
Now,
two halves of one soul and one body,
unknown to each other.

My things all over the room,
a date I never went to,
my youth,
stayed behind.

Harpstedt, Germany, 1995

This poem was part of a long letter Eleonora sent to the editors of The
Suitcase. *She wrote, "It is hard to describe pain with words. It just stays in
us like an eternal scar." Due to failures in the mail system, Eleonora's cor-
respondence didn't arrive until long after the manuscript had been completed. But somehow it found its way, and because it touched us so deeply
we decided to reopen* The Suitcase *and include it.*

Woman, 19 years old, Sarajevo
NO WAR!

Why are you crying, behind my back?
Yes, down there behind the black curtains of some forgotten stage.

Deep in your eyes, and not so long ago
I can see
extraordinary curtains painted with pure idealism.

Isn't it beautiful, even if they're not matching
my taste.
Or maybe my tears have another cause . . .
perhaps a love,
not surviving anymore.
Yes, I am suspicious . . .

Thousands of screams
sharing the same night,
sharing the same message,
NO WAR!

I know you simply cannot forget
nights with a full moon hanging on the sky,
and that you are waking up
with the taste of bloody victories and screams for help,
thousands of young souls
with the whisper of the same name on their lips.

Suddenly, you feel that all of those ideals are not so important
anymore.
Souls young and innocent,
victims of this bloody play.

Thousands of screams,
sharing the same night,
sharing the same message
NO WAR!

Islamabad, Pakistan, August 1994

*The author is now in Canada. This song was written for her dead friends
from Sarajevo. Before she shared this poem, she showed the photographs of
her friends. Sitting cross-legged on the floor at the Hajji complex in Pakistan, she pointed to photo after photo of smiling, long-haired boys. "It was
all of the hippies, the peace types that died," she said. "All of the boys with
college education and money got out as soon as they could. We were the ones*

who fought and died." Among the dead were the author's boyfriend and all of her best friends.

The author said that she doesn't hold a grudge against all Serbs. "But if I found the people who killed my friends and hurt my family," she swore, "I would kill them." She said that she's not sure how she could live in Sarajevo again.

*Wounded soldier of the Bosnian army, 30 years old,
and his wife, 28 years old, Zvornik*

PRINCESS ELEONORA

WOMAN: People in Serbia do not know the truth, they don't know what is going on there, they think that Muslims are doing terrible things. I am twenty-eight-years old and I came in 1994 from Zvornik. It wasn't difficult to get out. I went first from Zvornik to Tuzla, where I had nothing. My husband was already here in Vienna, released from the army because he was wounded. In Zvornik Serbians lived in my house and I lived in a Serbian house in Tuzla. We were all refugees in our own countries.

MAN: We work here without a permit because one cannot survive on humanitarian aid. There is no future for me here, there is no freedom here, there is everything except that. The law is very strict here for us refugees; I always wonder if I am permitted to do this or that. I am grateful to them for what they have done for us, but I am not relaxed. I make the children stay quiet, not disturb people, not to do anything that might attract attention. We are not used to this kind of life. Our children stay all day in the street and do whatever they want.

WOMAN: We would go back anywhere in Bosnia if there were peace. Lots of people are going back even to the war regions, to Tuzla. They live better there than here notwithstanding the grenades.

MAN: Before the war we lived all together. We were Bosnians. Then Arkan with his pack came and they started to shoot. There will be no peace until everybody goes back to his place and until they put away the leaders. We could live again together, all of us who didn't get our hands dirty. Justice will win. I was never a Turk, my religion is Islam, and I never chose my friends according to nationality but I listened to the soul. You can have enemies out of your same religion. We were all mixed in marriages and friendships.

I was a shoemaker, my wife is a housewife. Now we have three children. I was a musician too and I played together with Serbs at the weddings; we didn't care whose songs we played. In our town there were many Serbs who didn't want to take part in the war and who ran away. Those who stayed had to take part. Some of them wounded themselves on purpose so they wouldn't have to go to fight. A Serbian guy, a friend of mine, left when he realized what was coming and he wasn't ready to take part in that crime. He can always come back. If he doesn't have a house I will give him half of mine.

Our baby Eleonora was born here, she has a name of the world, and she has a bank account. She will get Austrian citizenship and all that we never had and all that we lost. She is our princess.

Vienna, Austria, May 1995

Refugees from all parts of ex-Yugoslavia are scattered throughout Vienna. Few are content; fewer still are on their way to becoming integrated. As in most other cities, refugees tend to live a separate life. Many refugees in Vienna saw the city as one big refugee camp with special laws for the second-class citizens: the refugees. They lived in small flats offered to them by the state, which they paid for — too much compared with market prices, they claimed — with their "refugee salaries." The state did not grant them permits to work or recognize their diplomas from back home. They saw no future for themselves, as if they had already "retired," but they still sought a future for their children, who were rapidly becoming Austrians.

They feel awkward with the strict Austrian way of life, and they complained of being indoctrinated into accepting a sense of inferiority. The wounded soldier of the Bosnian army said: "Every time my baby cries, I feel

*like I am disturbing the whole city. It seems like only our children scream
and cry, our children who used to grow up with everyone looking after them.
Here people are divided by family, flats, areas, languages. . . ." Still, he was
convinced that his child could only have a future in a new country.*

Radmila Bartel, 36 years old, Sarajevo

A PUPPET FATHER

I have three small children. The war started as far as I am concerned
very suddenly in Sarajevo. I was born in Dalmatia, my father is from
Bosnia and my mother is Dalmatian, but I was brought up as Yugoslav. That was my homeland. I always asked myself, where does
all this rage in people come from, to fight this war, and what is the
truth? They took my homeland, Yugoslavia, and I couldn't accept
Croatia as my new homeland. I couldn't even find my God because
I was a communist. I stepped out of the party but I didn't know to
whom to turn.

I was a social worker, like my husband. We helped people from
the beginning of the war and we felt useful. At a certain point I
realized that nobody could help me: I was watching the grenades
and killings but I couldn't move. I lived from day to day, happy to
stay alive. I decided firmly to stay on in Sarajevo. But one night we
heard that they bombed the Red Cross center where I was supposed
to be that night. It was sheer destiny that I survived. Then I decided
to leave even though I thought that it was safer at one's home, even
in Sarajevo, than on the road, in the bus which could be stopped. I
didn't even dare think what might happen. My husband didn't come
with us: we knew that refugees have no future, only sheer life.

A man in the bus paid for my ticket because I had no money. We
traveled to Gornji Vakuf where we stopped and they put us in private houses. These people who took us were fantastic, they understood us and, even though they were poor, they gave us all that they
had. Only in their eyes could I recognize that we were refugees.

There were military troops everywhere on the road; I couldn't make out which was which. In Sarajevo we were all taken aback by the war. My Serbian friends said: we are stronger, leave behind your Yugoslav illusions, the war will soon end, the Muslims have no weapons. But Sarajevo was all of us, Sarajevo has its own soul, I knew that the end of the war would not be soon. My husband stayed in the Bosnian army; before he had been in the JNA.

We came by bus to Split where my parents lived. My father was a JNA officer, a communist, Orthodox. Now he has lost his pension in Croatia. They live on Mother's pension and it wasn't enough for all of us. The poverty did not matter, but the fact that my view on Sarajevo did not agree with theirs mattered. My father would not believe me when I would tell him that I knew who attacked me. He just hoped that everything would pass by, but life hasn't stopped for me.

After the first moment of shock I started to think about the future of my children. In Split I was out of my mind, I had no normal life, everybody had a different opinion about the war and I realized that it was only a war of local factions: I couldn't sit and watch my cousins go to the front while their mother stayed home and cried, whatever side they were on. Then my children started to ask me: "Mother, who are we?" They had heard they were Croats now and that is when I decided to go to Vienna to my mother-in-law who was urging us to go there. My parents were against it, but I didn't like the atmosphere in Split. I wanted to go outside the war. I couldn't resolve the war, but I was the only parent to my children and I had the responsibility to save my mental health and to make something of our lives. I left my husband to fight the war in Sarajevo; this refugee life was my female way of fighting the war.

My mother-in-law had only one room, without a bathroom or a kitchen. She had no money so I decided that it was safer for me and the children to go to the camp for refugees. I went to one for mothers with children: sixty-two rooms, a wooden barracks. That summer I spent walking with the children through Vienna; I didn't have the money for the tram. But the children forgot the war and that they were far away from home. It seemed as if some future existed: the children will learn the languages, they will go to school. I started learning English and German too. The small possibility that existed for me was already a big opportunity. But still it is terrible to know that all of your life you have worked for nothing, that you have no more language, no more habits, nothing familiar.

My camp was closed in autumn. We were taken eighty kilometers away from Vienna. There was no possibility to get work, to learn a language, to go to school: I had a feeling we were cast out from the world, from all the happenings. I had no contacts with friends, with my family, and deep inside me I had a fear: I didn't know what to say to my friends; I was afraid of crying. I decided to wait for the end of the war and to meet them again. I was afraid of their unhappiness because I knew I couldn't help them.

When it became cold in the camp I had no warm clothes for my children. But I couldn't take anything from the Caritas Aid because it was my job to help other people. I remember the trick we used to make people take the clothes: we pretended we had brought clothes from home because they were too proud to take help from humanitarian aid. I felt the same way. But other women helped me and brought things for me. Clothes were in trash bags. Later I got used to that because I had no choice. Those trash bags with clothes were the only thing that happened to us: we could choose them, wash them, iron them, fold them.

I helped one woman with her housework but I couldn't take money from her; I've never done that. She helped me learn German and to ratify my diploma. I had to fight for my own language and to come back to Vienna. I finished a school for languages and I got a job in Vienna as a cleaning woman. I finished my diploma by passing an exam for which I studied in the tram. I managed to get a new job, as a social worker for old people. I even got a refugee flat for families.

I don't write letters to my friends because I have no words to express my admiration for their courage to stay in Sarajevo: I keep sending them something all the time but I cannot write.

My children now have everything they need. Before, when we stayed in the camp, they drew a house with many windows and their father standing at the window. Then I made for them a big rag doll which looked very much like their father, so they could play with him. They call him their puppet father.

Vienna, Austria, May 1995

Radmila, a lively woman with a warm sense of humor, has the will to survive and to help others. She works with humanitarian and feminist organizations in Vienna, and she helps refugees of all ethnonational backgrounds. She wanted to find a way to help the people of Belgrade too — "because they live under such bad conditions." Her husband left the Bosnian army a few months before she told her story. They live together in Vienna.

Croatian villagers living in Serbia and Krajina Serbs

NOBODY'S LAND: A CONVERSATION

HOST: They came to my door. Three people: a man and two boys. The man had a long beard and a uniform without any rank. They asked me if I could take them in. I am a Croat and my family has been living here for four hundred years. I accepted them. There are five of us and we have a small house. We gave them one room and we stayed in the other. We don't feed them; they eat at the Red Cross.

SOLDIER GUEST (40 years old, in torn uniform): We knocked on all the doors. This family was the first one who accepted us. My brother was killed three years ago in Sibenik and this boy is his son. I had to run from Sibenik to Knin and in Knin I volunteered to fight. My wife is somewhere on the road. I left Krajina when we had the order to retreat. I didn't manage to get home. The man who accepted us is a good man. I think I will stay for some time here and then I must find some other place. I wrote my name on his door so that it protects him. Other [Serbian] refugees won't come into the house to harass him. They know that he already has a family in his house.

HOST: For the time being we are getting along. I don't know what will happen in future; I don't want to leave this village, even though I am a Croat. I would rather die.

WOMAN (50 years old): My husband is a JNA officer. We are Croats, old inhabitants of this village. We took a family of Serbs from Krajina in with us. They have a small baby. We feed them. They had nothing when they came to us. We told them: "We will share everything we have until we don't have anymore." I don't know what will happen but we won't leave this place. It has always been our home.

MAN (refugee, 30 years old): I think you should leave this place and go to Croatia. The houses we left are much richer than the ones you have here. We cannot go back. The Croats would kill us and we have no place to stay here. We heard that the authorities are filling our houses with Croatians from everywhere. You should have those houses.

WOMAN (resident of the village): I am a Yugoslav, my sons are Yugoslavs, we stayed Yugoslavs after the war too, and we don't want any other country for our home. People of all nationalities are just Yugoslavs here in Yugoslavia.

SOLDIER: We shouldn't permit the war profiteers to ruin the image of all refugees. We are honest soldiers fighting for our country. We lost our country, we didn't lose only our houses. This Yugoslavia isn't our country. We can go now anywhere, abroad, it is the same for us.

YOUNG MAN (26 years old): I spent six months in Kerestinac [prison near Zagreb]. Since then I came here but I have nothing to live on. I heard that it's easy for us who spent time in prison to get visas for foreign countries. I must go somewhere and marry somewhere outside this crazy country.

ELDERLY MAN (resident of village): My brother left yesterday for Hungary. A gang came and beat him in front of the house just because he was a Croat. He already had Serb refugees in his house, but they wanted everybody out, him and the refugees. They wanted his house. So he left with his family. The Serbian refugees are keeping his house from these gangs. The Yugoslav police came and they ran away, but we are afraid they will come back. The police cannot be with us all the time. We are protected by our Serbian neighbors. A friend of ours came to stay with us and protect us. He is a Serb and his family is in a very similar situation in Osijek [Croatia], so he wants to help us. I don't want to say anything anymore; I am afraid. Everybody here is afraid, Serbs and Croats. Most of the refugees from Krajina are also desperate and afraid. We hope that the police will stop these gangs and bring us some peace.

Novi Banovci, August 1995

In August 1995, after Croatian troops recaptured Krajina, the break-away area of Croatia that had been Serbian-populated and Serbian-controlled, over 250,000 Krajina Serbs fled into Serbia. Some of these new refugees went to Croatian houses in villages in northern Serbia, demanding that they be accommodated. A number of Croatian families fled in fear. This is a recorded conversation between some of these refugees and villagers in Vojvodina, near the border with Croatia. During this tense stand-off, everyone was afraid of everyone else. Refugee and resident alike were generally unwilling to talk to the press, as they feared manipulation and distortion. Only through human contact did we manage to persuade them to speak.

The reference to "a similar situation in Osijek" was to the fallout of the JNA and Serb paramilitary attack on eastern Slavonia in the spring of 1992. Serbian families living in Osijek, Croatia, reported harassment by Croatian families who had lost their homes in Serb-controlled eastern Slavonia.

Milica B., middle aged, Sarajevo
GROUND WHICH IS NOT MINE

I try to avoid thoughts about the leaving day at the bus station in Sarajevo because it causes an avalanche of painful memories. During those first days of the war you had to be lucky to get a ticket for Zagreb. Although we went three days in a row to the station, I was praying to myself that I wouldn't get a ticket . . . and never go away from you. I felt like an intruder among all of those faces pained by a desire to leave a town which was about to become hell. Standing in that crowd of faces, we looked at each other in silence, letting people push in front of us in line. Together we watched a group of tear-stained children, mothers hustling children, self-confident fathers who still promised that they would fix everything. Children, especially those slightly older ones, were convinced that they were going to the seaside to visit relatives for a couple of days and after that they could come back to their rooms, kindergartens, schools, friends. They didn't know, and neither did I, that those visits were going to last two years and who knows how much longer.

A lot of things have changed since then. Almost everything. Here I am now, sitting in a rented room, watching through the windows an alien street, some alien faces, movements. . . . Even though I have been in this town for almost two years, deep inside myself I still keep the feeling of not belonging, exactly the same feeling as in those days when I first arrived in Zagreb. The feeling occasionally awakens and surfaces: a rude comment in the tram or simply any dear song from my life before the war and I remember I do not belong. Still, being in this city has given me a chance to find myself, to think of life and remember its real value.

I remember those first few days of refuge. Then I didn't know exactly what it could mean. A refugee, a subtenant, without a job, without hope. For days I was sitting in front of the TV waiting for brighter news. You called me every day; every day I used to think that I was going to spend the next one with you.

Everything started to become worse and look more hopeless after the phone lines were broken. It was as if somebody cut off pieces of the ground I was standing on and detached it from the piece on which you were.

The only way out was work. I gave up studying for a while and started to look for a job. Any kind of job. It was important to get out of the house, rebound, start to live no matter what. So I started to work in the kitchen of a fish restaurant. For eight, often nine hours, I soaked in the scent of fish and shells, cleaning squid, washing dishes. Two months later I quit because I could not endure the work; my spinal problems, which had been bothering me for several years, returned again. So I went back in front of the TV, absorbing each collection of news, which was becoming more and more alike every single day. And time was passing.

I wanted to do something that would bring me closer to people whose destiny is similar to mine, who share similar feelings. I wanted to talk to them, to support them. I wanted to get over my own feelings of being useless.

Sometimes I think that people always find what they are looking for and that nothing is an accident. But it seemed like an accident when I found a group of women working with women refugees. By working with those women, sympathizing with their desires and their suffering, I drew new strength for myself and found a new desire for life.

After two years of living far away from home, after everything that has happened in my town, and every other city in Bosnia, I realize how everything in life can be replaced by something else. After the rain the sun is coming; after the sun, rain; evil replaces good. I don't know where I am going to be tomorrow; I am not getting attached to places, streets, I don't have my own bench in the park. But I can say that I have managed well in my new surroundings. I have a job and that means a lot to me, and I intend to continue my studies, and I even have some new friends. Time is passing.

My biggest burden now is that I am so far away from you. Two years have passed since that day in the bus station. A lot of ugly things have happened, tears, sorrow, loss. Still, I believe in life. This time during which we are not together, we who love each other, is only a drop in our remaining time. And this terrible war is only a rain after which the sun will shine again.

Zagreb, Croatia, 1994

Women who work with refugees in Zagreb point to Milica as an example of a success story — a woman who survived. Milica came to the Center for Women War Victims as a client and became an activist at the center, leading workshops and providing services for other women refugees. She now lives in Chicago, where she still helps women survivors.

Rada Boric, 43 years old, Zagreb

THE OASIS

"I'm from Zagreb, Croatia."

"Croatia?"

"One of those countries of the former Yugoslavia."

"Oh, well, what has really happened there?"

"I can't tell you. I can only tell you of the things written on women's bodies and souls . . ."

Often when meeting foreigners I can see in their eyes a blink of astonishment, sympathy, or a wish to help. To ease their worried minds, I used to tell them that we hardly know all the hows and whys but that every day we are more and more aware of the whats of our war.

War. It doesn't only destroy houses and property and kill beloved ones. It wipes out entire landscapes of personal histories. Families are separated, friends have gone, either missing or cast out all over the world.

We are all born with the assumption that no one will do us any harm on purpose. At least not our neighbors.

Was it a mere nightmare? What is this war about? "Ethnic cleansing"? Who needs burnt-down villages? They fight for what? To devastate and then possess? To possess a house where some other life has been led? To have good dreams there?

When the first refugees came from Bosnia, some were placed in carriages in an old railway station from which trains no longer leave. A young girl, still a child, was washing train windows while two younger sisters cried in their grandmother's lap. Both parents had been killed. She was making a home for them.

Lost identity. White plastic bags containing all belongings. Old, yellowish documents, a few photographs.

I work in the Center for Women War Victims. War victims, or rather "war survivors." War has changed my life as it has changed many.

Now we talk about times "before the war." Before the war I was a professor of Croatian language and literature at the University of Helsinki in Finland. I was a visiting lecturer at Indiana University in the United States. Only then it was Serbo-Croat and Yugoslav literature. I had started working on a Serbo-Croat/Finnish dictionary. It made no sense to continue once the war started.

Work in the center has enabled me to see the world through the eyes of refugee women: I'm Mirsada from Sarajevo holding my husband's cut head on my lap during the shelling of my town. I'm Ruza from Derventa. I buried all my valuables under the plum tree in my garden, hoping to go back, but now I'm waiting for a refugee visa from Canada. I'm Mara, taken from a hospital to a Serbian camp. I'm Alija from Prijedor with my forged passport going to Sweden illegally with my two little children. Their father, my husband, is missing. I want to start a new life. I'm Badem, hushing my daughter in the tram, hushing her so the other passengers won't recognize that we are Bosnians.

I'm all of these women. I remember my friend Eve Ensler, a playwright from New York, saying that everyone should, if nothing else, be a refugee for a day. To feel the loss. To understand. To share. In a refugee camp you can still feel part of a community. Outside you are lost in a society that does not care.

My work in the center is my escape from the new reality. I am facilitating self-help groups for refugee women, trying to help them regain control over their lives. What about my life? Did I not need to regain control, to find identity—woman's identity?

These women fled from Bosnia or occupied Croatian territory with their children and parents, hoping that once they reached Croatia they would be safe. And now, after all of the atrocities that they have witnessed, after all of the traumas and all the resettlements, they face new problems.

Women and children make up 80 percent of the refugees. Jobless, their identity card entitles them to primary health care and primary schooling. Only the primaries. There are far too few places in the refugee camps, no money to pay for decent shelter. But they struggle. This is why I need to identify with them. They know how to survive. To start a new life when you are 52, 38, 67, 24 . . . to start a new life is to be a survivor.

I live in an oasis of caring refugee women—a place focused on helping each other become who we were or are. And I learn life's wisdom from them as we prove every day that women do not share hatred with each other.

Zagreb, Croatia, March 1995

Rada is one of the preparers of The Suitcase. *Rada, a professor of Croatian language, set aside her teaching profession at the start of the war to help form the Center for Women War Victims, a humanitarian group for women refugees and war survivors. This piece first appeared in* New Internationalist, *no. 270 (August 1995).*

Jasmina Tesanovic, 41 years old, Belgrade
REFUGEE IN MY OWN COUNTRY

It is like a constant pain you cannot localize: it's in your stomach, it moves up and down, and sometimes even takes away your breath or the ability to walk. There is an invisible wall around you, a wall of thin air made up of people's long looks at you. Looks which say, you are different, you move in a strange way, you speak and think as an alien, and we will judge you for that. We may even like you, which sometimes makes things even more complicated for you than if we don't notice you. You pray not to be noticed but then, if somebody just offers you a nice hello, you are ready to cry and tell him your life story. You give all that is left of you but you are not able to take anything: nothing can satisfy your hunger for home, for the loss of security. Even if you know that bad things have their other face, that the last will be the first, the unhappiness you feel buries your hope with a plain and calm indifference. This is the peace of survivors, who must be emotional cripples to have survived.

When I packed my few belongings, hurrying to get away with my daughter from Belgrade (which was supposed to be bombed at the beginning of the war in Bosnia), I forgot to put in the suitcase my diploma, which could get me a qualified job; my "permesso di soggiorno," which shows that I lived in Italy for more than ten years (and which could be renewed); and my daughter's birth certificate, which proves that she is my child since we have different surnames (so I could cross borders with her). Instead, I didn't forget books of Marcel Proust, lots of warm clothes in the middle of the summer, a scarf my dead aunt knitted for me, and my *I Ching* book. I read in search of lost time, I slept with the scarf under my pillow, and after my daughter would go to bed, I spoke for hours to my sage and ancient mute friend, who would often advise me: perseverance furthers; not eating at home brings good fortune.

I spent that summer in Vienna, once the city of my dreams, in desperate emotional loneliness, unable to see any of the beauties that city offered. When I spoke afterward to a woman from Sarajevo who was there that summer of 1992, going to the same places with her children as me, blind as me to everything but that terrible hum in one's head saying war, war, war, I realized that my experience too was a history: history of a sense of guilt, impotence and shame for what was going on in my homeland.

I watched TV news without understanding a word: I saw pictures of war and destruction, and I saw scenes of disorder in my city. I saw young people sitting in the parks, in front of the parliament, refusing to be mobilized. A clear thought struck my political conscience: if all those people left, just as I did, my city would be abandoned to those who will make us guilty for going away after they forced us to do so.

I packed up every single item I had brought and went back home. We set up a publishing house of women, women against war; we worked with refugees; we taught at Belgrade Women's Studies. We who stayed tried to defend civilization. In other words, the war, the crack in the system, opened a new space for us, a free space, never imaginable before when everything seemed all right. Our rulers had war business on their minds. We, the marginal ones, could press ahead with our squeaky little voices.

And only few months ago, a refugee Bosnian girl in St. Louis said to me, hearing that I lived in Belgrade: go away, they will get you as they did us, we also tried to stay to the very last hoping that good would win out over bad. And I shivered. That was the first time during this war that I realized how different are the similarities of refugees. And even though my persistence endures, I must admit that I am truly afraid.

Belgrade, Serbia, July 1995

Jasmina is one of the preparers of The Suitcase. *She wrote a book entitled* In Exile *during the first years of the war, as a matter of survival. "I wrote* In Exile *in my own room," she recalls; "I finally thought my writing was worthwhile: it was born out of the necessity to say and name things that writers I had admired until then had ignored." In addition to her work on* The Suitcase, *Jasmina has worked with women's groups against war in Belgrade and has cofounded the first feminist press in Serbia — '94 — which publishes feminist, antiwar, and multicultural books.*

Habiba Metikos, 50 years old, Sarajevo
CONVERSION

I feel a pain in my heart when the phrase "life in exile" come to my mind. You are interested in my life in exile, but I must mention the wonderful life I had before in order to compare my present and past life. I was an intellectual, I worked, I was married. I had a daughter and I lived in the most beautiful city in the world, as you guess, in Sarajevo. On the 11th of April my present painful life started. My twelve-year-old daughter and I left all that meant life to us. Some strange people broke our life as if it were a glass and we were just two pieces who had to set off to make up a whole someplace else. That day we could leave only by taking a plane to Belgrade. What a paradox! To be a refugee means to be driven from one's home, but then not all refugees are equal: Serbian refugees can to go Serbia, Croatian to Croatia, and Muslims, nowhere. I am one of those.

We came to Belgrade. I dared not pronounce my name because it is a Muslim name. War in Bosnia got worse and worse and my stay in Belgrade became unbearable. I decided to send my only and long-time expected child to my cousin's place in Canada. I went to Germany to stay with friends. Both of us could not survive together in one place because we didn't have enough money. I thought that conditions in Sarajevo would improve and that we would soon return. My husband stayed in Sarajevo. That day, May 9, 1992, was probably the hardest day in my life—that was the day when my child went out into the unknown world. I looked at the departing plane for a long time. It seemed that the little black dot in the sky would stay there forever.

Ten days later I went to my friends' house in Germany. I had met those people fifteen years ago at the seaside in my country. They had come to our place in Sarajevo, and now I came to theirs during the worst point in my life. Since I was not the rich lady anymore, they treated me differently. I worked in their restaurant, cleaning and cooking for eighteen to twenty hours each day, just for food and a place to sleep.

One month later, I decided to go away. The only place I could go was Zagreb because I had some relatives there. So I went to Zagreb. My child's life in Canada had become complicated, and I needed to bring her to Zagreb too. She did not have a round-trip air ticket, but a few kind people lent me the money and my girl arrived. Then, life took a turn for the worse. At that time, my mother died in Sarajevo. She was everything to me since my father had died when I was young. Her death was extremely hard on me. I couldn't call my husband at all, because the phone lines didn't work to Sarajevo.

In Zagreb, I again dared not pronounce my name because the only important thing was to have a Croatian birth certificate, which only pure-blooded Croats can get. That's how you can get work, a passport, and put your child in a school.

A Croatian birth certificate became my obsession. After a year I found a priest who didn't refuse to convert me and my daughter to the Catholic religion. I paid for it of course, because you cannot take on a new faith for free. I was infinitely happy; I thought we wouldn't be hungry and without clothes anymore; we had had nothing to live on until then. I swore allegiance to my new Catholic God, I forgot my Muslim one, who had brought me all that pain. But my birth certificate didn't bring me happiness because the name written on it wasn't Croat but Muslim. The authorities just spat on my one-year stain and I had nobody else to spit on but myself. I couldn't get a job because I wasn't a real Croat.

Our position became worse every day. I stood in line for clothes and food: we were fasting. And then God finally accepted the birth certificate of my daughter and we managed to put her in a school where people were more tolerant, maybe because she had a name which was universal and quite frequent in Croatia.

Wandering around, by chance, I came upon a women's center, for victims of war and violence. I started working there, helping other refugee women. And that is when the worst period of my life ended. I found myself in the women's organization and I found the strength not only to survive but to find myself. Those girls, Croatians, were like all other Croats except they weren't nationalists. They wanted to help every woman. I felt like a human being again and my faith in people was restored.

Zagreb, Croatia, and Winnipeg, Canada, 1995

Habiba is one of the preparers of The Suitcase. *Along with Rada Boric and with the support of Oxfam, she is organizing the group of refugee contributors and local women's organizations who will decide how royalties from* The Suitcase *are to be spent. Habiba counseled other women refugees at the Center for Women War Victims. After many complications, her family was reunited and now lives in Canada, where they are struggling to adjust to a new life. Habiba emphasizes that "this story is only one small part of my life as a refugee, because my story alone could be a whole book."*

THE ABCs OF EXILE

Dubravka Ugresic

efugees from Bosnia-Herzegovina and Croatia often long for what once was. Refugees from Bosnia-Herzegovina in particular describe their homeland in golden tones, romanticizing coffees in the town square with friends of all nationalities; hikes in the forests and walks through historic towns, exploring mosques, churches, cathedrals; eating grandma's pita and auntie's baklava. And refugees from Bosnia-Herzegovina and Croatia alike glow when they remember peaceful summers singing to the strum of guitars on the beautiful Dalmatian coast, sipping the best cappuccino in the Balkans when the sun went down. Those refugees of the thirty-something generation who find themselves now in Serbia weep when they see KiKi bonbons, a favorite candy from their childhood produced in Croatia and a symbol of all the little things blocked by war — little things that add up to a life. Refugees may lament the death of Yugoslavia, not because it was a perfect state or because they necessarily believe it offered a better alternative to a collection of smaller states, but because the flawed past offered more hope for life than the present war and than life divided artificially by ethnic groupings, an impossible operation for families spanning two or more ethnic groups, which is roughly half of the families in the largest cities in prewar Yugoslavia.

Many of these refugees speak of a feeling of exile, and some of being exiled in their own country, or at least in what had been until recently their own country. "I've pounded on the doors of every government organization I could find — I have to get out; I will die if I am in exile in my own country

any longer," exclaimed an ethnic Serb from Bosnia married to a Muslim.
The woman's son had just been kidnapped and killed in Serbia. "I went to
school in Zagreb, I considered it my home, and now I am in exile here, in
my home!" cried another woman from Bosnia, a Muslim woman who
teaches her children to remain silent on the streets of Zagreb to hide their
accent. These women live an un-life in an un-country, an exile that can
never be erased, no matter where they flee.

Dubravka Ugresic, a well-known writer, captures this feeling of exile.
Before the war, Ugresic's books were read and celebrated by people of all
parts of and all groups in ex-Yugoslavia, people now divided, displaced, and
exiled.

I have forty-five years and very few illusions. I belong to that number of four million ex-Yugoslavs who (with or without identity papers) wander within the borders of the ex-country or within the
countries that have only started to exist. I join the tribe whose scattered members at this moment are at every point of the map of the
world. I am *homeless, expatriate, exiled, refugee, nomad* all in one—a
person with the passport of a new European country. I know that
the bureaucrats are going to keep trying to persuade me something
opposite. Many words have remained the same, but the context and
time have changed. Their meaning doesn't correspond any longer to
their official duty.

Trummerfrauen—that is how women who cleaned the ruins after
the war in Germany were called. I pull just a few bricks out of the
ruins; behind me is a ravaged city, enough work for a lifetime. I
chew dust, I don't feel tired; as if hypnotized I stare into something
that once could have been called a house and I seek an answer to the
question, "How was it possible?"

I write down my trummer pages, words push each other nervously, every one of them only multiplies "impotence" or even "fal-
sity," just as Theodor Adorno, one of the exiled, already wrote a
long time ago. But still I don't give up, I interrogate until exhaustion.
Is hatred really the motor of everything? If that is so, where is the
heart of hate? In fear. If it is so, where is the heart of that fear? And

so on and one after another, like in fairy tales in which the hero passes seven mountains and valleys in order to conquer a dragon. And the dragon's force keeps transforming, now into one thing, now into another, now into a fish, now into a bird.

Sometimes it seems to me that the worst misfortune that can happen to a nation is that its *enemy* nation speaks its same language. The worst punishment that can happen to an *enemy nation* is that its victims speak the same language. The worst punishment that can happen to representatives of one nation is that both *the executioners* and *the victims* are theirs, that they speak the same language. In this hellish trick lies the beginning and the end; that is where all of the force lies, a road to the eternal, exhaustive clinch.

The builders of new states are accusing me that I am a nostalgic woman. My nostalgia has very unclear contours, it is physical, it is special. It is, it seems, mainly sonorous.

Sometimes when I meet a compatriot, I surprise myself in how pleased I am listening to his or her talk. I listen to the melody of the language, I don't mind what is being said. And he blushes for being recognized, I notice as he stops, as he pricks up his ears. Rapture is like being in love. Very often in the streets of foreign towns I steal towards my countrymen, I walk for some time behind them, I listen to their intonation, guessing where they come from. And now I think I know that language is our punishment, a pledge of remembering and forgetting at the same time, a pledge of our eternal, painful, and exhausting relationship.

Sometimes it seems to me that everything that nations[1] in the Balkans do is a constant effort to prove their diversity in comparison to the other. All forces are mobilized for the task: linguists and political scientists, politicians and historians, biologists and counters of blood groups, workers on the construction of national identities, masters

---

1. Translators' note: Urgesic uses the word *narod*, which literally means "nation," but it could also be translated as "people" (as in "people of a nation"). American readers should note that in Europe the term "nation" does not necessarily mean "country" but rather ethnonational group.

of make-up and disguise. That is why not much strength is left for everyday life. Sometimes it seems to me that nations from the Balkans are thrust into an oppressive, humiliating battle in order to prove their own identity, into an everlasting and terrible fixation in front of a mirror, into compulsory narcissism, into a painful construction of the history of personal absurdity. And from the mirror, instead of our own reflection, the OTHER ONE stares at us, our spitting image, dragging after us like a shadow. Constant worry for the national ego is a tiring job; nations get tired after a while, put down their arms, join together for some fifty years or so, take a breath, the hate heals up, and then they start all over again.

I often think that the hatred is a big lie, which was imposed as a universal truth by the masters of the war, knowing that it will be accepted enthusiastically by the political giants, institutions, and politicians. Because the truth I encounter when I travel, the people I meet in Madrid, London, Zurich, Antwerp, Amsterdam, Berlin, Paris, are of a completely different lot.

Some time ago I happened to be on a ship, a tourist ship (called the "Mayflower"!) in an evening sail on the Thames with around 200 young people from ex-Yugoslavia who were studying in Great Britain. During the three-hour trip we were remembering our ex-homeland. The new states, funnily enough, we didn't even mention. Young ex-Yugoslavs exiled from the hate test tubes as mature, serious, intelligent young people are sailing into a safe future even if now it doesn't seem so to them. At the same time, the Balkan nation ship of fools, carrying with it millions of people, is sailing into certain death.

I am forty-five. I am learning an alphabet. I am dealing with the first letter. N, as in Nobody. I was well scrutinized in the country of blood types, they have counted every one of my blood cells and written down everything. Before I was Everybody: Croatian, Slovenian, Bosnian, Serbian, Macedonian, Albanian, Montenegrin . . . Now I am Nobody. I refuse to be anything else.

I am learning the alphabet. Exile is a way of life. I learned to sustain a desire to buy certain things. Because out of all things, those of value have only a good suitcase.

I am trying to forget something. I am trying to forget the fact that not one generation in the Balkans manages to escape war, that in every family there is at least one killer and one killed, that new life only begins on somebody's dead head.

I notice some changes in myself. I now regularly cry when I watch movies in which justice triumphs at the end. Before I didn't cry.

Sometimes I am confused by the feeling that I am living a quotable history, as if I am a heroine of some novel written long ago. The sense of repetition does not diminish the authenticity of the emotion. The feeling that I belong to hundreds of thousands with the same story doesn't diminish my own personality. On the contrary, it seems to me that from that point, from the point of exile, the paths of personal destinies begin. Hundreds of thousands of refugee children are already chatting in the languages of the world. Exile is experimental teaching and advanced education.

On my corner, there where the west part of Kurfurstendamma ends, sits the Dresdner bank. On the corner, leaning against a wall, an old man in slippers is crouching and smoking. He is puffing imaginary circles of smoke, lost in his thoughts into the Berlin air. Bosnian, a refugee.

Sometimes in my apartment, I crouch too and mentally I join my compatriot. I examine the small object which I bought for 15 marks from the souvenir salesman at the Brandenburg gate. The souvenir, a patchwork under glass, contains several postcards from East Berlin (Brandenburg gate, the Wall, Potsdamer platz with the curving serpent of the Wall), an old stamp of DDR with a revolutionary motif, a few thin pieces of the Wall, an old DDR coin and a badge, red star with hammer and sickle.

I, a nostalgic woman, they say, moved by the purchased object, try to put together my own collage in my head, and suddenly it seems that there are the same amount of memories, just as little. Flags, parades, Tito, pioneers, hammer and sickle, folk costumes of nations and ethnic groups of people from Yugoslavia, the map of Yugoslavia, "a beautiful country on the hilly Balkans", the pine tree of Pancic, and the man's fish.[2] And look, the man's fish—that transparent endemic creature which looks like a salamander—is the only truly unique element of the collage. I remember how school buses with thousands of children left from all over Yugoslavia to see Postojna cave and man's fish. I saw it too. The fish has changed country and citizenship. Now it is Slovenian.

Recently some biologists near Zagreb discovered a unique example of fauna: a blue frog! During mating season, the unusual Croatian frog changes its color from green to blue. In my head I am already arranging the future souvenir collage of my new country, and look, there are a few possible symbols from which to choose: flags, coat of arms, Dubrovnik, map[3] of Croatia (where you have on the western side Italy, Austria and Hungary, on the eastern side a large gaping hole!), somebody's bust, somebody's picture, a little bit of geography, a snippet of history, a few technical inventions with the Croatian copyright . . . Pens, ties, the blue Croatian frog.

State constructions are so fragile and so little is persuasive. That is probably why millions of people must support it with their lives.

In my apartment, my temporary Berlin residence, I sometimes squat just like that, mentally joining my compatriots, now ex-compatriots. I am obsessed by one thought: I wonder how many lives, destinies, personal calamities, how much personal suffering has been invested so that in the end everything would fit into a small collage which can be sold for 15 marks.

In Berlin you find Teufelsberg, the highest Berlin hill, around 115 meters high. Underneath the grassy surface of the hill, 26 million cubic meters of the ruins of the city of Berlin pulsate,

---

2. The "man's fish" is a prehistoric fish that exists only in Postojna cave in Slovenia.

3. Translators' note: For "map," Ugresic, apparently ironically, uses a new Croatian word, *zemljovid*—literally, "the vision of the earth." Before the dissolution of Yugoslavia, the word for map used in Croatia was *mapa*.

dragged here after the war. I notice that lately I am walking through life as if walking over Teufelsberg.

I am learning the ABCs of exile . . . Dark-skinned Tamilians cruise the town at night offering roses, leaving sticky smiles everywhere behind them. At the entrances of the metro stations Vietnamese sell cigarettes. Near the Brandenburg gate Pakistanis, Ukrainians, and the Polish sell souvenirs of communism. At the Berlin flea market my compatriots are looking for small cheap objects which will help them make their refugee *heim* a home. Russians are advancing in western Berlin, they are opening shops on Kant Strasse and on Saturdays, in the restaurant of Berliner KDW, with champagne and caviar, they perform brunch. East and West are running into one another, everyone is learning some new alphabet. And at the end all the ruins will be covered by indifferent grass.

I am forty-five and I study the ABCs again. I am stuck in the present moment. I don't think about the future. The only solid thing that I own is a good suitcase. Sometimes it seems to me that it is the best thing that could happen to me in my life.

Berlin, Germany, October 1994

THE FACE OF WOMEN REFUGEES FROM MUSLIM COMMUNITIES: ALGERIA TO EX-YUGOSLAVIA

Marieme Helie-Lucas

C lose your eyes and imagine a woman refugee. Better yet, a woman refugee from a Muslim community or country. Is she cowering in some dusty street, crying over a dead father, brother, son, waiting patiently in line for the next handout, subjecting herself to the desire of male leaders, hiding her self, her dreams, her life? Newspapers seem to love such images of women refugees from Muslim communities and countries, lumping women from Bosnia-Herzegovina together with women from other Muslim communities everywhere in the world. Pictures of defenseless victims sell. They also distort reality.

Women and, in particularly large numbers, women from Muslim communities and countries, are victims of the war ex-Yugoslavia and other wars around the world. However, they are also survivors, as the voices in this collection attest. We asked Marieme Helie-Lucas, co-founder of the women's solidarity network Women Living Under Muslim Laws, to comment on the ways in which Muslim women have organized and fought back against oppression. The greatest struggle facing the world today, Helie-Lucas warns, is against fundamentalism, fascism's latest guise. Constructions of "Muslimness" have been used by all sides to fan the flames of fundamentalist-driven conflicts. She urges us to listen to the voices of refugees and to struggle against these forces, which are gathering steam not only in ex-Yugoslavia but in all countries and on all continents.

The only things I took with me when I left Algeria were my personal letters and photographs; those kept me alive for months and
years when I was still thinking of myself as one in political exile.
Now I can conceive of myself as a migrant, growing roots in another
country for good. However, we are reminded daily of the status of
refugees and exile; we hardly pass a day without seeing or hearing
about friends, or friends of friends, who have fled Algeria and
landed somewhere, desperately looking for a visa, a job, a little bit
of money, a room, a permit to stay, a school for their children, while
their beloved are still stuck in Algeria, murdered in that mad match
of fundamentalists and the state, using heads of people to chalk up
points, to fight against each other.

The situation in ex-Yugoslavia spoke to our hearts from the very
beginning; despite the different circumstances, we feel similar political forces operating in both our countries. These are the very
forces growing now all over the world, using religion, culture, and
ethnicity to divide people in order to gain political power. These
political phenomena are known as fundamentalism: they are the
new forms that fascism takes at the end of the century. We should
identify them as such and combat them in whichever specific form
that they take in each of our countries. If we do not, one even wonders where one could seek refuge. Religious Islamic fundamentalism in Algeria, in Iran, war in Somalia, ethnic massacres in Rwanda,
ethnic and religious fundamentalism in Pakistan, ethnic cleansing
in ex-Yugoslavia, Hindu fundamentalism and extremism in India,
fundamentalists of the Christian right in the United States, racism
and the rise of the extreme right in Germany, in Italy, killings in
Cambodia, in Kashmir, and so many others . . . No continent is
spared.

I salute the resistance of so many people from ex-Yugoslavia who
still refuse to be identified merely by ethnicity or "national groups."
We are witnessing now the rise of identity politics, which creates
subnational and transnational groups, antagonistic to and exclusive
of one another. At the same time the international women's move-

ment is reclaiming our multiple, concomitant, and nonantagonistic identities: on the one hand reconciling within ourselves the gender, national, cultural, race, class, beliefs, sexual orientation, and other elements of our identity; and on the other hand trying to acknowledge and respect our differences with one another as well as building on our commonalities. What fundamentalists (be they ethnic, cultural, or religious) are trying to do is to impose a single, forced identity.

Fundamentalists create the Other, who is then portrayed as the enemy. In Algeria, we were made Muslims by the law of the state, and it is the West which is the external enemy; any questioning of any aspect of that which is imposed on us as women in the name of religion is seen as a betrayal of community and religion, as collusion with imperialistic powers. In ex-Yugoslavia, one witnesses the creation of "Muslimness" both by the fundamentalist Serbian government and by fundamentalist Muslim groups operating within some of the relief programs they organize. The mere acceptance by the international community that Algerians or Yugoslavs or Pakistanis can all be referred to alike as "Muslims" is outrageous. Deliberate confusion between what can be the personal faith of a person and such a transnational identity aims at establishing for "Muslims" the same place in the world that "the Reds" once occupied for a long time in the imagination of many people: the absolute Other and Enemy.

This construction denies us the right to agnosticism and atheism or to choose other beliefs by virtue of place of birth and ethnic or national origin. This is not unimportant at a time when the revival of religions benefits fascisms. In ex-Yugoslavia of all places, where so many people had not been believing Muslims for generations (at least no more than all those who have a party for Christmas are Christians), "Muslim" has now become a nationality, with the blessing of the international community!

This is to me a clear political indicator of the weakness of antifascist forces in Europe. Because of the history of colonialism and for fear of being accused of racism, the Coward Left in Europe allows its "white guilt" to dominate its political judgment and leads it to support the most horrendous practices (such as female genital mutilation, forced marriages, or stoning to death for adultery) in the name of cultural relativism and freedom of expression for all cultures. The same trend is to be observed in human rights organizations, which see less and less problem in the free and public expression of racist calls for murders, such as those of the Muslim fundamentalists in Algeria and the Hindu fundamentalists in India, or in the fatwas of Iran and Bangladesh.

Muslim fundamentalists and liberals in Europe participate together, wittingly or unwittingly, in this political manipulation. Aziz Al-Azmeh wrote a powerful and lyrical demonstration of this "Machiavellic bastard crossbreeding" of what he calls the bizarre holy family. On the Islamic side, we see radical and internationalist Islamism appearing either as populist fascism or as worldwide culturalism tied to activist organizations and ex-leftist intellectuals willing to assert a freshly acquired cultural virginity; on the Western side, we see tenants (be they secular, priests, or rabbis) of the "exotic integrity of an imaginary Islam." Their discourse on exotic identity produces "a savage identity, composed of archaism and immutability, deprived of hope and modernity—a homogeneous identity, One, identifiable, 'Other.'" [1]

This identity discourse blurs "the force and ubiquity, the reality of struggles in all countries with Muslim majorities . . . between religious reaction and enlightened critical thinking." Through this peculiar grid of misreading of their imaginary Islam—more Catholic than the pope—the "bizarre holy family" of Muslim fundamentalists and liberals in Europe turns their "barbarity" into the very essence of their authenticity; it becomes "their authentic self, their historical maxim, the limit of their historicity, the essence of their

---

1. Aziz Al-Azmeh, "Rushdie the Traitor," in *Pour Rushdie: Cent intellectuels arabes et musulmans pour la liberté d'expression* (Paris: La Découverte, 1993).

incapacity." This "arrestation of history, or its 'hijacking,' amounts to the confinements of others to existence as 'cultures.'"[2]

Facing this enormous wave of fundamentalism, women have undertaken a heroic resistance. Far from being helpless victims, women from Muslim countries and communities are at the forefront of struggles against fundamentalism, occupying the entire spectrum of activities, in the Arab world, in Africa and Asia. They have nothing to lose and everything to gain: fighting fundamentalism is a question of life and death for them. Women undertake systematic exchanges of information in order to strengthen local women's groups and to link them into networks to increase their efficiency at national and international levels. They negotiate with political parties, elaborate alternative propositions for legal reform, denounce the collusion of religion and patriarchy, challenge fundamentalist interpretations of religion, set up collectives of lawyers to support women who dare make challenges in court, and organize legal literacy programs for women.

This nonexhaustive list of activities undertaken by women activists in the Muslim world is a far cry from the situation of women's organizations in the West, as well as from the image of "Muslim" women propagated outside our countries. Last year French women were discussing how to improve the way women are treated in police stations when they come to report rape, violence, abduction of children, etc. I suggested that they should contact Indian women's groups for inspiration—these were among the first women to initiate women's police stations led by women police officers and to organize gender-sensitive training for all police officers. Another women's group in France was debating setting up a women's party or a women's trade union. I suggested that they should contact the Pakistani women who started the first women's trade union in Karachi over five years ago. I wish we had, where I now live, one of

2. Ibid.

the three women's lawyer collectives they have in Lahore, or one of the twenty-odd activist women's organizations covering all forms of activities they have in Dhaka.

While so many European countries denied refugee status to ex-Yugoslavs—themselves Europeans—because of the "barbaric character" of their imposed "Muslimness," other Europeans accepted as logical the notion that the Bosnians be deported to Asia or Africa, that is, where the other barbarians live. The fact that Pakistan or Libya accepted Bosnian refugees in solidarity with their Muslimness is not unambiguous. On the one hand, the refugees at least escaped from dangerous areas; on the other, the receiving countries obviously had a political agenda for opening their doors. In the absence of alternatives, fundamentalist organizations have been taking over humanitarian relief and social work in many of the receiving countries, regardless of whether the destinations are Muslim, with the blessing of the "host" governments, who are just too happy to ignore growing poverty and unemployment and while our official lefties, who are too busy with their politician politics to spare time on unproductive "charity," wash their hands of the whole business. It should therefore be acknowledged that the left too is responsible for the making of fundamentalism with all its particular consequences for women.

Women are the primary targets of fundamentalists. As properties of men and the state, women are violated, seized, abducted as part of the spoils of war. They constitute the majority of refugees in all wars and in all conflicts, in any location in the world, and now the majority of women refugees are "Muslim." The horrendous stories told by women refugees from ex-Yugoslavia are no different in essence from those told by women who escaped fundamentalism in Algeria (where women are abducted, raped, tortured, beheaded, and cut to pieces for un-Islamic behavior), or those of the 1971 liberation war of Bangladesh, which left 300,000 women raped and impregnated by the occupying armies, or from the stories of the "comfort women" abducted and reduced to sexual slavery in camps by the fascist Japanese army.

But the time has come for international resistance and solidarity among women. The "comfort women" of World War II have taken the Japanese state to court; they have already received official apologies from the Japanese government and are negotiating the payment of monetary compensation. Over the last few years, on all continents, women have held public hearings, not only in their countries, but also collectively on the occasions of United Nations world conferences, such as the Conference on Human Rights in Vienna in 1993, the Conference on Population and Development in Cairo in 1994, and the Conference on Women in Beijing in 1995. More and more women victims of armed conflicts and of war crimes are organizing to use national and international legal instruments to bring their oppressors to justice. Moreover, they now share their experience and technical expertise across national boundaries by calling meetings where their lawyers confront brutal methods and activists support the cases internationally. Through such actions, women challenge the de facto immunity that war criminals still enjoy. The common actions of the international women's movement will, in the end, become a persuasive voice. We know that women from Muslim communities have been the primary victims in ex-Yugoslavia; however, women from other communities have been victimized too, and it is collectively, as women victims of all wars and all patriarchal societies, that women will demand justice and reparation. The voices of survivors have been heard by many women throughout the world.

My last word will be for Women in Black and the S.O.S. Hotline in Belgrade, dissidents of dissidents, working in the heart of the beast like anti-Nazis did in Germany sixty years ago. They endlessly cooperate with all women refugees, breaking cultural, ethnic, and religious boundaries, promoting tolerance and solidarity, fighting fascism and militarism. For this they face attacks by fascist Serbs and harassment from the Serbian government, which even attempts to forbid them from entering refugee camps. Alongside the voices of refugees, we must hear these voices too: they stand in Belgrade week after week, for the honor of humanity, reminding us that each

BEYOND THE BALKANS

Judith Mayotte

W e care about the voices in this book because they are all of us, all of humanity. While these stories are from those who have fled Bosnia-Herzegovina and Croatia, refugees and displaced people around the world tell similar stories of flight, loss, dreams of home, and attempts to start life anew. The context and circumstances of their struggle change as we move across the globe; many refugees in other parts of the world face additional struggles of endemic poverty, lack of development and health care, and other problems that existed long before the conflict began and that complicate and impede their ability to flee, to survive in exile, to return, or to begin life again elsewhere. Still, some chords in refugees' stories are similar. A call for dignity. A call for visibility. A demand for a chance to live in peace.

We asked world-renowned refugee expert Judith Mayotte, who has traveled on numerous fact-finding missions to hundreds of dwellings of refugees and displaced people in Africa, the Middle East, Asia, and Europe, to draw some of the chords together, to remind us of the millions of other voices not included here. Even after witnessing unspeakable human suffering and even after being wounded herself during her work in the war zones of Africa, Ms. Mayotte has maintained hope that we can somehow move beyond the Balkans, Rwanda, the southern Sudan, and put an end to the problems that force refugees to flee in the first place.

To tame the savageness of man and make gentle the life of the world.

AESCHYLUS

The voices in this book reach far beyond Bosnia-Herzegovina to the millions on every continent who have become refugees or internally displaced civilians. They speak for Rwandans, Burundians, Armenians, Azeris, southern Sudanese, Burmese, Guatemalans, Peruvians, Tamils, Tibetans, Kurds, Somalians, Algerians, Tajiks, and so many more who have been uprooted from their homes and traditions and fled for safety either within the borders of their homelands or beyond to a neighboring country of asylum. They have lost all they possessed, even a sense of self.

"We have lost the picture of ourselves. We have lost the pictures of ourselves." A young Bosnian woman in refuge in Mostar spoke these words, dropped her head, and became silent. There was nothing more to say. Her companions nodded.

To lose the picture of yourself is to lose your spirit, your soul, your self. These women, like millions around the world who have been forced to flee their homes to survive, wanted to reclaim what was theirs in the depth of their being. A fifteen-year-old's story tells it best. I will call her Emina. Although her small town in eastern Bosnia-Herzegovina was predominantly Muslim in population, Croats, Serbs, and Muslims lived peacefully together. Emina loved going to school and dreamed of becoming an engineer or an architect. Then everything changed. "It happened so fast," Emina recalled. "One day we lived together peacefully, and the next Serbian soldiers, some of whom were our neighbors, dragged us from our homes. Many of us women were violated in front of our families and neighbors before we were taken to the schoolhouse and imprisoned. Many of our fathers and brothers were killed." Bosnian Serbs took Emina and her mother and sisters to the gymnasium along with some 250 other women and girls. Others were crowded into classrooms. The soldiers abused and raped them over and over until one day, several months later, they were freed in an exchange of prisoners.

Some of the women took a circuitous route to Mostar. They sought out a physician they knew there, a gynecologist who had once lived in their hometown and had assisted at the birth of many of the women's children. A wise man, the doctor knew the women needed to deal with the brutality they had experienced in an atmosphere of trust. Only then could some of them begin to reveal what had happened.

When I was alone with Emina, she took a plain white sheet of paper and began to draw. What she showed me was an architectural rendering of the school building. At the far right end was the huge gymnasium. A hallway connected it to the rest of the school and all of the classrooms where she had learned mathematics, languages, history, science, and art. In the same building where her dream to be an architect or an engineer had emerged, her dream was shattered. But in that sketch, as professional as any architect's drawing, I could see the dream was still alive. Emina was struggling to capture the picture of herself.

Emina and other women and girls in her town were persecuted because of who they were ethnically. Bosnian Serbs targeted them as Muslims, as civilians, and as women. While all "sides" have raped in the war, human rights researchers have found substantial evidence that Bosnian Serbs used rape strategically, as a weapon of war. Rape became part of a military strategy to terrorize and cause Bosnian Muslim civilians to flee their homes. In all too many of the more than forty conflicts raging in the world today, the exploitation of racial, religious, tribal, and linguistic differences abounds. Civilians, who are no longer observers of war, are bombed, terrorized, starved, persecuted, or made to flee because of who they are ethnically, racially, politically, religiously, or due to what they believe, or by reason of their gender.

A Rwandan Tutsi woman, who witnessed women and girl children being raped in front of family members, neighbors massacred with machetes, and who survived the slaughter, asked, "Why was I born a Tutsi?" She lost everyone dear to her because of who she was ethnically. In areas of conflict, millions of others ask, Why was I born a Muslim? a Jew? a Hutu? a southern Sudanese? a Palestinian? an Afghan? a Socialist? a woman?

Neither internally displaced civilians nor refugees who have crossed the border into a neighboring country to find safety have a sense of security—particularly women and children, the vast majority of the dispossessed. All live on the edge in a constant state of fear. A southern Sudanese woman said to me, "We are tired of running—running from bombardments, massacres, and starvation. We take our children and try to find a place of silence. Sometimes we hide in the bush for months. We look for water and try to stay a while. But guns break the silence and we have to run again."

In the past forty years since independence in 1955, Sudan has had only one eleven-year hiatus from a civil conflict that has claimed the lives of more than a million southern Sudanese civilians and the disruption of the lives of the other five million. At least 85 percent of the southern Sudanese have been forcibly displaced from their homes; many have been dislocated several times. The withholding of food and medical supplies has been used as a brutal weapon of war by all parties to the conflict. Hundreds of thousands of civilians have starved to death or died from preventable diseases.

A group of midwives I met in the Nimule area told me they did not even have clean razor blades with which to cut the umbilical cords in the birthing process. In the same area, two doctors and five nurses, serving a displaced population of 125,000 southern Sudanese, functioned with few supplies and little medical equipment and felt helpless in the face of so many malnourished and dehydrated displaced people. In a small one-story structure that served as a hospital, mats crowded together covered every available floor space and served as beds for hundreds of critically ill patients. Outdoors in the dusty courtyard, children too weak to brush flies away waited for death to release them from their emaciated bodies. Members of the medical staff were aware that they could not stem rampant diarrhea, for they lacked a remedy as simple as therapeutic oral rehydration solution. Disease spread more easily since the only source of water, a river, was used for bathing, washing clothes and utensils, and drinking.

Only when the Sudanese government allowed humanitarian organizations to resume relief operations could the situation change. To this day assistance reaches civilians caught in the conflict only intermittently and is frequently interrupted by government orders or callously intercepted by combatants on both sides.

For these and millions more internally displaced civilians around the world there is no protective United Nations convention like the 1951 Convention Relating to the Status of the Refugees and the subsequent 1967 Protocol, nor any UN body with the mandate to assist and protect them. In fact, Article 2 of the UN Charter prohibits any form of foreign intervention in the internal affairs of a sovereign nation. Nothing, it says, "contained in the present Charter shall authorize the United Nations to intervene in matters which are essentially within the domestic jurisdiction of any state or shall require the Members to submit such matters to settlement under the present Charter."

In the case of southern Sudan the international community is grappling with the complex issue of the conflict between national sovereignty on the one hand, and humanitarian access to and the protection of the human rights of the internally displaced on the other. Sovereignty, until recently, has usually been regarded as sacrosanct, as absolute, no matter the determination of a "sovereign" government to eradicate by genocide a certain segment of its population. No matter that a state implodes as Somalia. No matter the genocide we witnessed in Rwanda and Bosnia-Herzegovina. Yet, by trying Germany for "crimes against humanity" against its own civilians, the Nuremberg war crimes tribunal opened the door to international scrutiny of how a country treats its own people. And by crafting a UN Convention against Genocide which applies in all circumstances, regardless of whether a conflict is international or "internal," the UN said *nie wider* (never again) to genocide. But we watched it happen in Cambodia, and we are passively observing it again today.

The international community is faced with hard questions. Are there basic human rights such as access to food, water, shelter, clothing, and medical assistance that cannot be violated, particularly when the denial of such rights is used by a government to eradicate a segment of its population? Can a government punish with impunity its people for being who they are—ethnically, religiously, or racially? Do other nations have a responsibility to act? Sovereignty carries responsibilities, not solely privileges. Is there a point beyond which a government cannot be permitted to go in abusing those citizens it is bound to protect? [1]

Sudan's war seldom makes the front page or the evening news. Its victims are hidden. But other wars have come into our living rooms and have brought us face to face with incalculable human suffering. In 1991, following the Persian Gulf War, we were numbed when we saw a sixty-mile stretch of humanity, two million Iraqi Kurds fleeing Saddam Hussein's forces, inching through mud and relentless rain into the rugged northern mountain terrain that divides Iraq from Turkey and Iran.[2] Even that did not prepare us for what we saw in Rwanda in the spring of 1994. Many people had not even heard of this tiny nation in Central Africa.

What we came to know because of Rwanda is that 500,000 Tutsis and moderate Hutus could be massacred in the short span of less than two months because of who they were ethnically. Hutu extremists exploited latent tensions between Tutsi and Hutu to such a degree that even churches where civilians sought refuge became slaughterhouses. Women, children, and the elderly, the most vulnerable of any fleeing population, were cut down with machetes in a house of worship. Elsewhere, bodies thrown into rivers stiffened and

---

1. Judith Mayotte, *Disposable People? The Plight of Refugees* (Maryknoll, N.Y.: Orbis Books, 1992), 260, 303.
2. Ibid.

bleached out in the sun as they tumbled downstream over swift waterfalls into Lake Kivu.

But when the war turned against extremist Hutus and the Rwandan Patriotic Front marched into Kigali, Rwanda's capital, Hutus ran for their lives. In just four days, between July 14 and 17, 1994, nearly a million Rwandan refugees, mainly Hutu, made their way to the Goma areas of Zaire. More followed, swelling the refugee population to at least two million. Never had there been an exodus of that magnitude in such a short space of time to such an uninhabitable area. A rocky and desolate volcanic place, it was almost impossible to gain access to adequate, potable water or to dig latrines to ensure necessary sanitation facilities. People bathed, washed clothes, defecated, and drew drinking water from Lake Kivu, a lake in which dead bodies floated. A sea of people on the move with many dropping beside the road to die was all there was to be seen. It proved difficult to dig graves in the volcanic land, and people were dying so fast that bodies lay in piles decomposing. It was a human disaster and a public health nightmare. As relief workers performed triage, they realized that many of those receiving their assistance were participants in the massacre of ethnic Tutsis that had touched off their cataclysmic tragedy.

In this upheaval, as in others around the world, women, children, and the elderly made up the bulk of the refugee population and suffered more. Early on, clinics were established to receive the sick. Inequities in refugee goods and services arose. It was the strongest who pushed forward for food and water and the strongest who received clinical care. Only through outreach programs could weaker members of the refugee population be served. However, it was not unusual that community leaders listed only male refugees when international aid workers sought out the very sick.

Among many refugee populations, women are either ignored or treated as more expendable than men. However, women are not expendable and, in fact, have their own needs. Women refugees and internally displaced women have witnessed children, husbands, and relatives being killed. In flight, many have been injured or maimed while others have survived imprisonment, torture, and sexual assault. In exile, many women face not only the loss of a spouse but also the prospect of being the sole adult in charge of their family. Addressing the protection needs of women is critical, particularly protection against sexual violence, exploitation, and discrimination as well as protection in assuring access to food and assistance. Attention to women's comprehensive reproductive health and needs is critical to the survival of refugee populations. And investing in the education and skills training of refugee and internally displaced women strengthens the whole community.

Children displaced by war have their own particular needs. Children often watch as their parents are being killed or become separated from them as they flee in search of safety. In the Kakuma camp in Kenya, near the border of southern Sudan, a sign reads: "Caution! 16,000 Children, Go Slow!" Most of the children in Kakuma are young boys who became separated from their families and who have survived a harrowing journey from camps in Ethiopia to Kakuma. As they trekked toward Kenya, many died from government bombings as well as from starvation and disease.

These children are identified as unaccompanied children, and their numbers are legion. They learn to fend for themselves. In the countryside and in cities such as Addis Ababa, Khartoum, Phnom Penh, Kabul, Kigali, Mostar, and Sarajevo, they stick together and at night they huddle to keep warm. All of them are deprived of essential foods necessary for physical and mental growth, and most of them are deprived of education as well. Yet, stunted from a lack of food and education and traumatized as they are, they are the future of their countries.

Training for and impressment into the military of young boys is widespread. Millions of children caught in the throes of war learn very early the concepts of war and the enemy rather than lessons in peace and friendship. A picture of a Liberian boy, not more than twelve years of age, is fixed in my mind. He stands tall in his military uniform, shouldering an assault rifle almost as big as he. This child was forced to kill his parents and some of his neighbors before he marched into battle.

I once asked a young Afghan student in his tent classroom what he would like to be when he grew up. He answered tellingly: "If I grow up, I would like to be a doctor so I can help those who are wounded in the war." He did not venture to say, "When I grow up . . ."

Children of war are never given time to be children. Many do not have the energy or have been too traumatized to play. They know and have seen too much for their young years, as I learned from a young boy not more than seven or eight years old, on a bombed-out street in Mostar. His name was Nenad, and on that rainy day he held a large, broken, black umbrella above his head. My interpreter asked Nenad if he was afraid of the war. When he replied that he was not, she asked him why. He said with great certainty, "Because our soldiers protect us." "Who are your soldiers?" asked the interpreter. "The Croatians," responded Nenad. The interpreter came back with a question, "But are you not Serbian?" Standing tall, Nenad said, "I am only a child and I do not know about such things."

If we do not want to witness one humanitarian crisis after another, each seemingly more brutal than the one preceding, we must be bold in setting new priorities and principles. Violent upheavals of massive proportions will continue unless and until we find new, nonviolent ways to respond to conflict situations. We can meet the challenge these upheavals present, but we would do well to bear in mind John Updike's words of caution: "An old world is collapsing and a new world is arising. We have better eyes for the collapse than for the rise, for the old one is the world we know."[3]

We have lived long in a war and weapons mentality. While we know our past is past and that we cannot change it—cannot disinvent the weapons we have made, disavow the wars we have fought,

---

3. This John Updike quote was used as an introductory page of a book put out by the Carnegie Endowment for International Peace. Carnegie Endowment National Commission on America and the New World, *Changing Our Ways: America and the New World* (Washington, D.C.: Carnegie Endowment for Peace, 1992).

deny the disharmony in so many parts of the world, we can shape
and create the future we dream of if we change the way we think
about and act with each other.[4] In reshaping our future, one of our
greatest challenges today is to work for reconciliation between war-
ring parties and among civilians caught in the conflict and to help
them find other ways to settle their differences apart from killing
and destruction. Although we have not done well in preventative
diplomacy or conflict resolution in Somalia, Rwanda, southern Sudan, Bosnia-Herzegovina, or Croatia, no one wants to see what
has happened in those countries happen again. Many nations stand
on dangerous precipices—Burundi, Zaire, Nigeria, Macedonia, to
name a few.

The transformation of South Africa could serve as a heartening
prototype. South African leaders and ordinary civilians saw the vio-
lence and inhumanity of apartheid taking the whole nation down.
Resolution and reconciliation came about not just because Nelson
Mandela and F. W. de Klerk came together to work out a solution.
It came because of the dedicated and unflagging efforts of thousands
of ordinary South African people who, through the National Peace
Accord launched on September 14, 1991, embarked on a peace process that gave a time and a tenable climate for negotiations. Susan
Collin Marks, a South African who was part of that process from
the beginning, recalls that it "encompasses the country and stretched
from top to bottom of society. . . . [It] provided a safety net without
which the negotiation process would not have been able to proceed.
. . . I shudder to think what would have happened if the peace structures around the country had not been there absorbing the daily
conflict and violence, defusing explosive situations, healing torn
communities and in many cases literally standing between a fragile
equilibrium and chaos."[5]

4. Ibid., 1, 77.
5. Remarks by Susan Collin Marks, U.S. Institute for Peace, Washington, D.C.,
April 15, 1995.

More than 20,000 South Africans were trained in the art of mediation and negotiation and tens of thousands of peaceworkers went out to build bridges throughout all regions of South Africa and on all levels of society. As Marks notes, although the work was dangerous, the peaceworkers forged ahead and helped the protagonists discover each other's humanity. Through such a constructive process, the people learned new ways to respond to conflict and difference. The paradigm shifted from the acting out of dominance and power to a process of collaborative, participatory problem solving. "What took place was nothing less than the transformation of the hearts and minds of people."[6]

There are many, myself included, who have walked among too many refugee and internally displaced populations, in too many war zones, past too many human remains not to turn our efforts to conflict resolution and crisis prevention. Symposiums, conferences, and meetings abound. But only in the field and on the ground can change occur. In Washington, D.C., for example, a working group comprised of people from government, international organizations, and nongovernmental organizations—both advocacy and relief and development—has the objective of preventing another Rwanda from happening in Burundi.[7] Ultimately, it is an effort to help Burundians help themselves bring about change by means other than violence, to find solutions to long-standing differences, and to reconcile. While meetings take place in Washington, the real work of the agencies and organizations represented in the forum takes place in Burundi. Most important in prevention is providing a climate of trust and patient, quiet diplomacy, both at the highest levels of government and at the grass roots. U.S. government and United Nations officials participate in high-level meetings in Bujumbura

6. Remarks by Susan Collin Marks, U.S. Department of State, April 15, 1995, and U.S. Institute for Peace, April 13, 1995.

7. The Burundi Policy Forum is founded under the auspices of Refugees International, Search for Common Ground, the African-American Institute, and the Council on Foreign Relations, Center for Preventive Action.

with members of the Burundian government while nongovernmental and grassroots organizations, indigenous and expatriate, reach out to people in the countryside. As with the efforts in South Africa, the purpose is to find common ground where people can air their differences and envision a way wherein they can move beyond what divides them. The process is long and arduous; it cannot be time-bound, limited to a week, a month, or a year. Progress is not easy to document except insofar as the country has not plunged over the precipice.

At no time has the coalescence of government, international organizations, and nongovernmental organizations been more critical to encourage and facilitate such work. When I walked among the ruins of a number of war-torn nations, I became tangibly aware of the centuries it takes to build a culture and a nation and the few months or years it takes to obliterate the land and the people who gave spirit and life to that particular culture and nation. Many of these wars need never have been, particularly had early warning systems been in place and had there been a commitment on the part of the international community to the art and practice of preventative diplomacy and peace-building.

A number of nations are now experiencing a cessation of war for the first time in years. Endings require new beginnings. The aftermath of war in countries like Cambodia, Mozambique, Angola, Eritrea, and Ethiopia is devastating. The infrastructure is in ruins. But changing strategic interests and domestic economic woes in donor countries may offer little hope that sufficient money will be forthcoming in rehabilitating land and lives.

Walking away from the ruins of these nations is neither in the international community's strategic or economic interests nor is it morally acceptable. Substantial assistance now will encourage the development of economically viable economies and self-sufficiency, as well as the cessation of residual internal strife.

Structural rehabilitation is but one aspect of peace-building. No returnee will go home the same, nor will the nation to which he or she returns ever be the same. Every person and every place will have been radically altered by the experience of war, exile, and the decimation of structures and land. Most refugees and internally displaced civilians will return to villages that no longer exist or that others have taken over in their absence. There will be land disputes unless provision is made for settlement and compromise. Families who fought on opposite sides will be estranged. Whole areas will be uninhabitable until millions of antipersonnel mines are cleared.[8]

People who come home have to find ways to live in peace and trust with their neighbors. In cases where massive genocide, rape used as a weapon of war, and other brutalities have been employed, reconciliation can only truly occur when justice is brought to bear. But even this is difficult to achieve when, as in Rwanda, most of the judges were killed or fled and the government does not even have pencils, paper, or desks. War crimes tribunals and truth commissions must address the worst wrongs and bring the chief perpetrators to justice. Only when this is achieved can a respect for justice and the rule of law take root and flourish.

Above all, we must go further than conflict resolution and crisis prevention to deal with the political, social, developmental, environmental, and economic situations that compel people to leave their homes. It is time to focus on the potentially dire consequences for nations when rapid population growth and a lack of sustainable development are combined.

The world's population is growing by one hundred million every year, adding the equivalent of Mexico in that time span or the equivalent of China every ten years. Overpopulated areas are the most prominent in the poorest nations in the world—some of which have become wellsprings of discontent and violence. Many developing nations experiencing rapid increases in population do not have the means or resources to sustain the growth and feel the strain that

8. Mayotte, *Disposable People?* 303–4.

high population density places on the economy, environment, government, and social fabric of the country. Overpopulation and underdevelopment lead to environmental degradation and land and forest abuse, economic disparity and deprivation, and, ultimately, the movement of people. Millions who can no longer survive on the land move to already crowded urban areas where a lack of housing, employment, and sanitation and a general erosion of living standards fuel social and political unrest. Others cross borders into other nations.

Without population stabilization and sustainable development, combined with crisis prevention and conflict resolution, our world is not secure—we are not secure. It is in the strategic, political, and economic interests of all countries in the world to address these issues. Moreover, it is a humanitarian imperative. Yet, in the United States, for example, only one percent of the federal budget is allocated to overseas funding. Substantial foreign assistance is a small investment to make toward enabling populations to live fruitfully in peaceable and secure homelands—and not to have to flee to survive. Ignoring or turning our backs on foreign aid is far more costly in the long run in the loss of lives, lands, structures, and the breakdown of societies.

To understand that without action we are not secure and that to act is in our self-interest requires that we break old modes of thinking and forge new ones. Realizing that all peoples are intimately connected, we can no longer act from a vantage of power but out of leadership and collaborative action. Together we can change the ways we think and act and move toward creating sustainable peace and development. But we can do this only if we believe that we belong to each other as sisters and brothers who are "riders on the earth together."[9]

---

9. Archibald MacLeish, *Riders on the Earth* (Boston: Houghton Mifflin, 1978), xiii–xiv.

POSTSCRIPT

THIS IS NOT WAR TALK

Julie Mertus

"In central Bosnia today, when you really want to insult some-one, you say, 'Da Bog da te UNPROFOR branijo a UNHCR hranijo.' Literally translated it means, 'May God give you the protection of UNPROFOR and may you be fed by UNHCR!'" Beba stared in stony silence at the UNHCR officer. He looked back at her intently, hoping to see a trace of a smile. No, this lady was serious. She certainly was not the grateful refugee he had hoped to greet.

"We used to believe in the United Nations; we thought you would help us," Beba spit the words out with distaste, "but now you tell me what to think."

The officer recoiled. The other Bosnian refugees gathered in the sterile Zagreb office looked down at their shoes. If you really want to help us, Beba continued in so many words, you would get the hell away from us. "We are so tired," Beba later confided; "we keep going somehow, but we are so sick of all of this."

When the war machines crank up again and UN troops again fall in the line of fire, refugees throughout all of ex-Yugoslavia become "sick of all of this."

Lifting the arms embargo. Bombs dropping on Zagreb. UN offi-cers held hostage. NATO strikes. Escalation of conflict. Shelling of Knin. Croats retaking lands occupied by Serbs. Muslims retaking lands occupied by Serbs. Serbs taking over safe areas. We're gaining territory. We're losing territory. Territory.

Clickety clack. War talk. Am I new to this, or is something missing?

I'm walking alongside another line of humans running for their lives. Tractors pulling carts piled high with blankets, baby clothes, bicycles, farm tools, families; buses with children peering through the sparkling holes where windows once were; women and men in flip-flops pushing tiny East German and Russian cars; a black Mercedes crammed tight with cardboard boxes; soldiers walking barefoot. This line is the largest single refugee flow in today's Balkan war: an estimated 200,000 to 250,000 people crossing the border to Serbia—nearly the entire population of Krajina, the self-proclaimed republic of Bosnian Serbs, which has been recaptured by Croatian forces. The distinction between refugees and retreating army blurs. Men in uniform accompany nearly every family, husbands and sons who had been ordered by their commanders to go home and take their families to safety. "I was so excited to fight the war when it all began," sighs Braco, one five-year veteran, "[but now] I will throw away my uniform as soon as I have some clean clothes." "Nothing worse could happen the rest of my life," his mother adds, cradling her two-year-old grandson in her arms; "I had over one thousand nut trees in my garden, six pigs and a wonderful house, but I could leave everything except my children."

The refugees who make it into Belgrade regroup at the fairground where buses await to whisk them away to the south. One elderly woman refuses to get on board. "During the trip my younger son was lost somewhere in the convoy," she cries. She had been sleeping on the cement for three days. "I will wait one hundred more days until I find my son." The refugees testify again and again that their leaders had promised them that the Yugoslav army would come and save them. "We were supposed to protect our land," says Dragica, a young woman lugging three bags of humanitarian aid; "but when the time came, we were sold by our leaders." She adjusts the bow in her girl's hair: "She was wearing practically nothing. I just picked her up and started running. Someone on the road gave us some clothes." Three young men in humanitarian aid sweat suits protest loudly: "We could have defended ourselves if we had a chance."

War talk? Clickety clack.

One month earlier: I'm sitting in the recreation hall of a Bosnian refugee group in Osijek, Croatia. Refugee women are supposed to be exchanging ideas on managing refugee handicraft projects. We have picked a bad day for discussion. The women press close to the television screen. They're looking for relatives. Thirty to forty thousand people streaming out of Srebrenica. A woman screams. She thinks she has spotted her sister. "Well, at least she's alive," sighs a young woman with dark crevices under her eyes. An elderly woman cradles the crying woman's head in her hands. "Did you hear? NATO bombed THEM?" a young man asks excitedly. A woman in a flowery print dress rushes into the room, "I just KNEW they would TAKE Srebrenica," she exclaims triumphantly.

Territory? Clickety clack.

I'm having dinner in Zagreb with some Muslim refugees from various parts of Bosnia-Herzegovina. The band in the pleasant outdoor garden plays a loud folk tune. Recognizing the song as an old Dalmatian favorite, the women begin bopping in their seats. Two large tables filled with men belt out the words, swaying back and forth, beers thrust high as punctuation points. The Bosnians turn pale and abruptly stop moving to the music. "I don't think we can endure this band," one of them says. I am so stupid. The tune was the same, but the men had changed the words from something about "beautiful Dalmatia, we love you" to "Dalmatia, never will you be Muslim."

Clickety clack.

Four months earlier: Refugees streaming out of recaptured parts of Croatia testify about bodies lying on the side of the road. "They threw shells at us as we ran." If given enough time to complete their story, they speak also of relatives, colleagues, friends, the ones who stayed on the other side of town, who will always be separated from them. The young men who made it to Serbia are particularly afraid. They refuse to go to Serbian-occupied parts of Bosnia-Herzegovina or Croatia. They vow not to fight. Police in Belgrade patrol the streets, check the bus station, clean out cafes. Trucks wait for human cargo. Men born in Croatia or Bosnia-Herzegovina are shipped back. We must regain. Territory.

Clickety clack.

Six months earlier: I'm bringing milk to an elderly Muslim couple hiding in an old house in Kosovo/a.[1] After Serbs killed their son and took over their home, they fled to Hungary, but conditions were so bad in the refugee camp there that they accepted a Kosovar Albanian's offer to take them back into Yugoslavia. The border guards let them in without papers. "After all, they're old. They look like your relatives from the village," explains the nervous worker at the underground Merhamet group in Serbia. "Their village [near Foca] was totally 'cleansed,'" he adds; "these people saw terrible things." When we enter, the old man and his wife are lying on dirty mattresses on the bare floor. "If you really wanted to help me," the old man pushes himself to his knees, "you would shoot me right now."

Clack.

Eight months earlier: Bosnian refugees in Germany, Switzerland, Norway, Sweden gather in church basements, hide out in cellars, change the names of their children. Their reluctant "hosts" have directed them to return home. Free one-way tickets are theirs for the asking. Parts of Bosnia-Herzegovina have been declared safe.

---

1. *Kosovo* is the Serbian spelling of this region, which is 90 percent ethnic Albanian and 10 percent ethnic Serbian. Kosovo had been an autonomous province of Yugoslavia until Serbian president Slobodan Milosevic pressed for constitutional changes in 1989 that stripped the region of its autonomy and made it part of Serbia. *Kosova* is the Albanian spelling of the self-proclaimed independent state of Kosova—an entity which had been created by ethnic Albanians in opposition to Milosevic's move, which they argue was illegal. To date, the controversy over Kosovo/a still simmers.

"Do they think we WANT to be HERE?" a humiliated mother of three wonders. "I've tried all of the human rights groups," a quiet refugee in Switzerland flatly reports; "they say it's not a human rights issue as long as the proper process is being observed." Process. Safe territory.

Clack clack.

Twelve months earlier: I'm sipping Bosnian-like coffee and eating Bosnian-like bread with Bosnian Muslims in Pakistan. After Muslim-Croat conflicts flared over territory, Croatia had given them forty-eight hours to get out of their refugee quarters on the Dalmatian coast: over four hundred people, most of whom have already spent a year in refuge, many of whom had lost family members or been imprisoned themselves in concentration camps. And Pakistan was the only country that would accept them. Because of their Muslimness. No other country had an interest in their well-being. "I want to be an airplane," a five-year-old boy whispers, "and fly my family back home."

Click.

Sixteen months earlier: I'm taking women refugees to coffee in polished Zagreb cafes. Business as usual in this cosmopolitan city now flooded with humanitarian aid dollars; talk of the town is the new underground shopping mall, built in the early days of independence by a wealthy Canadian expatriate. We speak one by one. Nearly all of the women speak of having seen other women being raped. "They did it on the street and everyone watched. No one did anything." "I hid in the forest." "I keep dreaming of her screams." "The smell of liquor on their breath." The women miss their families, worry for the loved ones left behind, fear for their children growing up with accents in a strange city. They never mention themselves. They never mention territory.

Cli -

Eighteen months earlier: I'm visiting a kindergarten run for refugee children in Zagreb. One boy misbehaves terribly, slugging at the other children, pulling the hair out of dolls, throwing himself on the floor in a tantrum. His teacher shows me a series of hand puppets that she uses with the children. "Most of them spent a month in cellars while their town was being bombed. That's quite traumatizing for kids," she finishes off with a wonderful understatement. "These kids were all in Vukovar when Serbian forces and the Yugoslav army bombed it into the ground." I give the kids some crayons; most kids draw pictures of their peaceful life back home, a few draw scenes of war, the misbehaving boy chooses red and black to scribble madly on the lime-green wall.

Cli - ck.

UNPROFOR carefully plots the war on black and white maps, complete with notations for front lines, recent military flares, safe areas, and other necessary information. Human rights groups, humanitarian aid organizations, foreign journalists collect those maps like souvenirs. I see them plastered all over office walls, from New York to Geneva to Zagreb. What if the printer suddenly made a mistake and instead of the zigzag front lines, the map sprouted faces? The faces we see on our television screens running away from Vukovar, Foca, Srebrenica, Knin . . . humans on the territory.

Clickety clack. You must be new to this. This is not war talk.

Belegis (village in Vojvodina), August 1995

NOTES ON CONTRIBUTORS

REFUGEE AUTHORS

Many preferred to remain anonymous, as their situation at the time of writing was precarious and their future uncertain. The refugee contributors range in age from five to about sixty-four; the vast majority are women. Some are professional writers; others had never written anything before in their life. All ethnic groups from the former Yugoslavia are represented. The editors and voluntary assistants traveled to all parts of the former Yugoslavia and throughout Asia, Europe, and North America in search of contributions. In addition, the editors solicited authors through electronic mail bulletins, refugee organizations, and women's peace groups. Authors were asked to write only about what happened during and after their journey out of their home town. If they also wished to write or testify about human rights abuses and other crimes that occurred before they left, the editors forwarded these sections of their stories on to human rights organizations collecting and assembling such data. Out of the hundreds of submissions collected, only a fraction are printed here. Information about individual refugee contributors is included in the editorial commentary at the end of their stories.

EDITORS

JULIE MERTUS, a writer and professor, is a fellow at Harvard Law School. Formerly counsel to Helsinki Watch and a recipient of Fulbright, MacArthur, and Soros Foundation grants, she is the author of *Our Human Rights,* a women's human rights education book that is being translated into several languages, and of *National Truths,* forthcoming from California, on nationalisms and Kosovo. She has written numerous general interest and academic publications and has taught law and policy at New York University, Cardozo Law School, Smith College, and the University of Bucharest (Romania).

JASMINA TESANOVIC is a freelance writer and translator who now lives in Belgrade, after spending fifteen years in Italy. She is the author of two collections of stories—*The Invisible Book* and *In Exile*—and an anthology of Italian contemporary literature. She has translated the works of Hannah Arendt, Karen Blixen, Joseph Brodsky, Elza Morant, P. P. Pasolini, Italo Calvino, and others. She has a weekly column of literary reviews in the daily *Borba* and teaches creative writing at Belgrade Women's Studies. In 1994, she founded the first feminist publishing house in Serbia—'94.

HABIBA METIKOS is a lawyer from Sarajevo. She came to Zagreb as a refugee in 1992 with her adolescent daughter; her husband stayed in Sarajevo. In Zagreb, she was unable to practice her profession and her daughter faced many difficulties in school. She joined the Center for Women War Victims in Zagreb, where she worked as a facilitator for self-help groups in the refugee camp Kruge (in Zagreb). She sent her daughter to school in the United States and began the long process of trying to relocate elsewhere. After many complications, the family was reunited in Winnipeg, Canada, where they have become refugees once again.

RADA BORIC, a professor of Croatian language and literature, is an activist in the Center for Women War Victims, Zagreb, Croatia. She facilitates self-help groups for refugee women in refugee camps and on the center's premises. A longtime women's rights activist, she is a cofounder of Women's Studies in Zagreb and a member of the Anti-War Campaign in Croatia and the Zagreb Women's Lobby. Ms. Boric has been active in many efforts to support the voices of women refugees and to break down barriers between women in all countries of the former Yugoslavia.

FOREWORD AND AFTERWORDS AUTHORS

CORNEL WEST is one of the most celebrated thinkers on mo-
rality and community in the United States today. A professor of
Afro-American studies and political science at Princeton and Harvard, Professor West's latest book, *Race Matters,* is an acclaimed
best-seller.

DUBRAVKA UGRESIC, a celebrated novelist, commentator, and literary scholar, was born Kutina (Croatia) in 1949. She is the author
of two books for children, *The Small Flame* (1971) and *Philip and
Little Luck* (1976); a book of literary theory, *New Russian Fiction*
(1980); and several works of adult fiction and essays: *Prose for Prose*
(1978), *Steffie Speck in the Jaws of Life* (1981; translated into several
languages and made into a popular movie), *Life Is a Fairy Tale*
(1983), *Fording the Stream of Consciousness* (1988; recipient of a major
Yugoslav literary award), and *American Fictionary* (1993; translated
into many languages). Ms. Ugresic lives in Zagreb but spends much
of her time in Germany and the United States, where she teaches
modern Russian literature.

MARIEME HELIE-LUCAS, who was born in Algiers in 1939, now
lives in Europe. She is the founder of Women Living under Muslim
Laws, an influential international solidarity network through which
women from Muslim countries and communities exchange information on the development of their situations and generate support
among themselves. She studied philosophy and sociology at the University of Algiers and social anthropology at the London School of
Economics and Political Science. She taught at the University of Algiers for more than ten years and in 1975 was one of the founding
members of AAWORD (Association of African Women for Re-
search on Development. She established Women Living under Muslim Laws after she left Algiers in 1982.

JUDITH MAYOTTE is an award-winning television producer, writer,
and refugee advocate. She has worked with numerous groups of
refugees, including the Cambodians in Thailand, the Eritreans, the
internally displaced Sudanese in the Sudan, and the Afghans in

Pakistan. Her book, *Disposable People? The Plight of Refugees,* was published by Orbis Books in December 1992. She was appointed to the U.S. Department of State Bureau of Population, Refugees and Migration in 1994 as a special advisor on refugee issues. She has been a senior fellow of the Refugee Policy Group of Washington, D.C., the chairwoman of the Women's Commission for Refugee Women and Children, and has served on the board of Refugees International and the executive committee of the International Rescue Committee. In 1994, for her work on refugees, Ms. Mayotte received the Refugee Voices annual Mickey Leland Award.

Designer:	Nola Burger
Cartographer:	Bill Nelson
Compositor:	G & S Typesetters, Inc.
Text:	11/14.5 Granjon
Display:	Agency Bold
Printer:	Haddon Craftsmen
Binder:	Haddon Craftsmen